COLLINS GEM

HORSES & PONIES

PHOTOGUIDE

Deborah Gill

Consultant: Deborah Cook

D0318341

HarperCollins*Publishers*

HarperCollins Publishers
PO Box, Glasgow, G4 0NB

First published 1996

Reprint 9 8 7 6 5 4 3 2 1 0

ISBN 0 00 470974 8

Created and produced by Flame Tree Publishing, part of
The Foundry Creative Media Co. Ltd
The Long House, Antrobus Rd, Chiswick, London W4 5HY

Special thanks to John Dunne

Printed in Italy by Amadeus S.p.A.

Contents

Introduction

Horses came to domestication comparatively late. Dogs had been settled by man's fireside since the Stone Age, but the first horse came to be tamed only around 6000 years ago. At first they were providers of milk, meat, and hides, but the advantages to a warrior of being on horseback quickly became apparent and the value of the horse soared. Without horse-drawn transport and the speed of communication it brought, mankind could not have started down the long road to civilization.

Today horses play a major role in our society, with competitions of all kinds, harness racing and hunting all popular, pony-trekking an increasing holiday choice, and many working horses on our streets and farms. Racing, and the breeding of racehorses, is a massive international industry, generating enormous amounts of money and giving pleasure to millions. All over the world horses are used for ceremonial duties and as police horses – in fact, India has more mounted police than any other country.

How To Use This Book

This book details a wide variety of information about
Horses – everything from facts about breeds, life-cycle
and breeding, to grooming, showing, famous horses and
classification. A series of photographs illustrate each topic.
The book is divided into six sections, together with
The Compendium at the end.

Each part is colour-coded for easy reference. Part One
which appears in green, presents general information
about the horse, including colours, points, markings,
anatomy and reproduction. Part Two is colour-coded
pink, and provides information about horse
classification. Part Three discusses horse management,
including learning to ride, basic schooling, buying a
horse and saddlery; it is coded blue. Part Four discusses
Ponies, including their role in history, and an in-depth
analysis of the breeds. Part Four is coded yellow. Part
Five, coded lilac, presents an in-depth discussion of the
Light Horse breeds. Part Six, coded a deep green,
introduces the Heavy Horse breeds.

Parts Five and Six provide all the essential
information you will need to know about breeds around
the world. You'll find details of the breed's history and
country of origin, and there is a breed basics box which
presents practical details of the horse: for example, its
use, size, colours and identifying features. Part Seven
features wild and feral horses and is coded orange. The
Further Information section supplies interesting extra
information about that breed, or simply horses in general.

The Compendium contains useful information on general aspects of horses, from world records and basic breeding, to law and horse health. There is also a handy list of addresses of various horse organizations, and a Glossary explaining terms which might be unfamiliar. At the end of the book you'll find an index which lists every subject and type of horse found in this book.

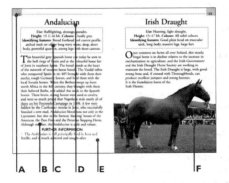

A The page number appears in a colour-coded box which indicates which part you are in.

B Essential information about the breed appears in a concise and fascinating introductory passage.

C Breed Basics list all the important details about a breed.

D The title of the chapter, in this case the breed name, appears at the beginning of every new section.

E Further Information provides interesting extra information about a breed or horses in general.

F The topic covered on this spread will be illustrated with clear photographs.

ALL ABOUT
HORSES

Evolution

Sixty million years ago, in what is now the state of Wyoming in the United States, a little creature died. It had lived in a world of tropical forest and marshy pools, reaching up for soft leaves to eat. Its skeleton next saw the light of day when it was discovered in 1867, nearly intact, in Eocene rock formations. The little creature was called Eohippus, which means 'Dawn Horse'.

Its ancestors were the Condylarths, the precursors of all hooved creatures, which existed about 75 million years ago. At 30cm/12inches high and with a rounded back, Eohippus was about the size of a small dog. It walked on four toes on its forefeet and three on its hindfeet. The species spread into America, Asia and Europe over the land bridges which existed at that time between the continents, until about 40 million years ago it finally became extinct.

The slightly larger Mesohippus was the next to arrive on the scene, about 35 to 40 million years ago. The Mesohippus was now walking on only three toes on its forefeet, which has led scientists to conclude that the environment was changing, with the ground becoming firmer and less marshy, and tropical forest giving way to scrubby, temperate-zone woodland. The Miohippus, bigger yet at 61cm/24 inches high, was next to evolve.

Then about six million years ago, in the mid-Pleistocene period, came the Pliohippus, the true prototype of Equus, and the first fully-hooved horse. Standing on the central toe of three, the toenail has now become the hoof as we know it. Pliohippus, much larger at about 122cm/48 inches high, also looked recognizably like a modern horse.

- Pliohippus also probably arose in America, spreading across the land bridges to Europe and Asia.
- Pliohippus is the direct ancestor of the four related types of Equus living at the end of the Ice Age, about 9000 BC:
  - in Europe and Western Asia the horse developed
  - in Africa the asses and zebras arose
  - in the Middle East the onagars arose
- Pliohippus became extinct 8000 years ago, and horses were not seen in the Americas again until the Spanish Conquistador Cortes arrived in Mexico in 1519 with a complement of 16 horses.

History of the Horse

At the end of the Ice Age, 9000 years ago, there were four types of primitive horse to be found. Three of these are the ancestors of our modern breeds.

- **Forest Horse:** heavily built, with broad feet and a coarse shaggy coat, the Forest Horse is now extinct, but lives on in today's amiable heavy horses.
- **Steppe Horse:** the Steppe Horse had a large head with long ears, a strong short body, and a mane with a distinctive hogged appearance. The Steppe Horse survives as Przewalski's Horse, or the Asiatic Wild Horse, the only truly wild horse still in existence.
- **Plateau or Desert Horse:** the Plateau Horse still exists as the Tarpan, which itself has been brought back from the brink of extinction using its modern relatives. With its small head, light body and long legs, the Plateau Horse is the ancestor of today's light horses and ponies.
- **Tundra Horse:** the Tundra Horse lived in north-east Siberia. Horse remains have been found alongside mammoth bones in the Yana Valley, and the modern Yakut pony, which lives in the same area, is thought to have descended from it. The Tundra Horse seems to have had no influence on equine development south of the Arctic Circle.

At the time when the horse was beginning to be domesticated, 6000 years ago, these primitive horses led to a further four discernible types of horse.

- **Pony Type 1** – Evolved from the Plateau Horse or Tarpan, Pony Type 1 is thought to have lived in

north-west Europe. The modern equivalent is the Exmoor.

- **Pony Type 2** – Resembling the Asiatic Wild Horse, Pony Type 2 lived in northern Eurasia. Its modern equivalent is the Highland Pony or Fjord.
- **Horse Type 3** – Horse Type 3, probably descended from the Tarpan, lived in central Asia and was a desert horse with a spare frame and fine skin, resistant to heat and drought. The Akhal-Teke or Sorraia is the modern equivalent.
- **Horse Type 4** – This horse, also influenced by the Tarpan, lived in western Asia and also became resistant to heat and drought. It was smaller and lighter, and may be seen as the prototype of the Arab.

Since the horse has been domesticated, the three main foundation breeds have been the enormously prepotent Arab, the Barb, and the Spanish Horse. These three breeds are genetically dominant, and their influence is to be seen in nearly all the light horse breeds of the world.

Today the principle divisions in the equine world are between:

- heavy horses, known as coldbloods
- light horses, known as warmbloods (Arabs, Barbs, and Thoroughbreds are known as hotbloods to indicate their unique purity of line)
- ponies (breeds and types below 15 hh; but proportion is also taken into account)

- A breed refers to horses registered in a stud book.
- A type refers to a horse which is not of fixed
  conformation, e.g. polo pony or cob.

Colours

The various coat colours of the horse world are governed by genetics. Each cell in the horse's body contains two genes, one from each parent. One of these genes is dominant, one recessive; it is the dominant gene which will prevail in the offspring. There is a fixed order of dominance for colour, with grey dominant over all other colours. After grey come in, order, bay, brown, black, and chestnut. Thus two black horses will produce a black foal, but a black crossed with a grey is much less likely to do so.

Colour is important for some breeds, although conformation and general health are always considered even more important. Spotted horses such as Appaloosas or Colorado Rangers, or horses such as Palominos or Albinos, are known as 'colour breeds'. These unusual colourings are the legacy of the early Spanish horses, although the modern Spanish horses do not have spotted coats, and neither do Arabs, Barbs, or Thoroughbreds.

SOLID COLOURS

- **Grey** Black skin with white and black hairs. Variations include Flea-bitten Grey and Dapple Grey.
- **Bay** Red-brown coat in various shades with black mane, tail, and legs collectively known as 'Black points'.
- **Brown** Mixed black and brown hairs with black mane, tail and legs from knee and hock down.
- **Black** Black hair overall, sometimes with white markings.

- **Chestnut** Various shades of golden brown, ginger or reddish colour. Variations include Liver Chestnut and Red Chestnut.
- **Dun** Black skin with yellowish hair, sometimes with dorsal stripe. Black points and sometimes 'Zebra' marks on limbs.
- **Roan** Black skin with coat of solid colour mixed with white. Variations are Strawberry Roan; Blue Roan; Red Roan.
- **Palomino** Golden coat, flaxen mane and tail. No white markings on body, though white is permitted on legs, with black or brown muzzle.

PART COLOURS

- **Spotted** Often called Appaloosa colouring, though not all spotted horses are of the Appaloosa breed. There are five patterns: blanket, marble, leopard, snowflake, frost (white speckling on dark background). Skin is mottled pink.
- **Piebald** Black skin (only under black coat), large patches of black and white. Two forms: *overo,* a solid colour base with white patches, and *tobiano,* a white coat with solid colour patches.
- **Skewbald** Large patches of white and any colour except black.
- **Pinto (Paint)** American term meaning either piebald or skewbald.

Points of the Horse

The points of the horse are its external features, which together make up its conformation. The conformation determines the breed of the horse. Horses are expected to conform to certain proportions, which are also good indicators of an animal's general qualities and state of health. If the conformation is weak there is an increased risk of disease and joint problems.

The right conformation is an essential factor in the work to which the horse is put. A well-made horse, performing a task for which it is conformationally suited, will perform better and for longer.

'Points' are mane, tail and legs from knee and hock down. Points are always black.

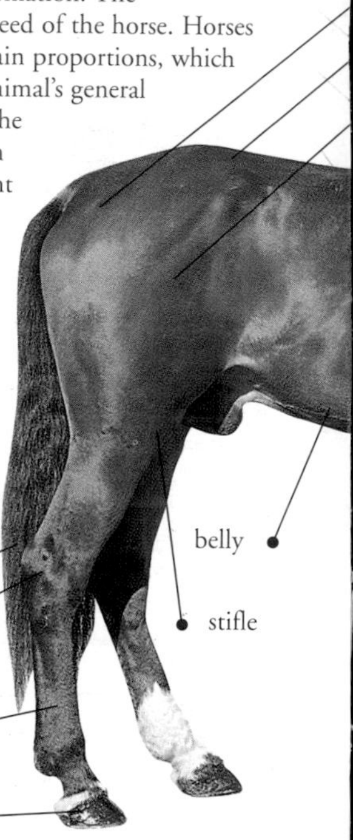

belly

stifle

tail

hock

shank

ho

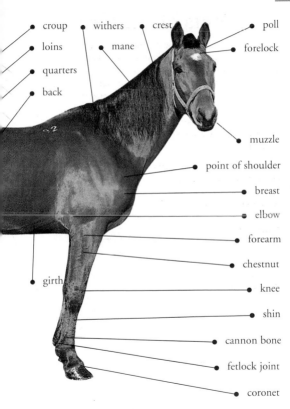

croup

withers

crest

poll

loins

mane

forelock

quarters

back

muzzle

point of shoulder

breast

elbow

forearm

chestnut

girth

knee

shin

cannon bone

fetlock joint

coronet

Markings

A variety of markings make each horse different from the next, helping with recognition and prevention of theft.

Man-made markings are brandings, either by hot iron or by freezing. Both these processes stop the hair growing back and create a permanent mark. The brand can denote ownership or identify the horse in some other way. Many breeds of horse have unique marks, often branded in a prominent position such as the shoulder. Some breeds have only one mark, such as the edelweiss mark of the Haflinger; whereas the Lipizzaner has four marks – the stud brand, the ancestral brand, the foal brand, and a plain 'L'.

The natural markings of the horse are areas of a different colour from that of the background, and can be very distinctive. A pedigree horse's markings will usually be carefully documented in its papers.

On the face:
- star
- stripe
- blaze
- white face
- white muzzle or mealy muzzle
- snip

On the legs:
- stockings (white, up to and over the knee)
- socks (white, up to the knee)

- ermine (black spots on white markings around the coronet)

On the body:
- zebra markings (rings of dark hair on legs, primitive in origin and useful for camouflage)
- dorsal stripe (almost always found with a dun coat. Both dun coat and dorsal stripe are of primitive origin and are still to be found in the Asiatic Wild Horse and Tarpan)
- flesh mottling (usually found with part-coloured coats)

On the hooves:
- blue hoof: slate-blue horn
- white hoof: white horn (usually found with white socks or stockings)
- striped hoof: found with spotted coats

Gaits

Most horses use the four paces which are natural to the species as a whole. These are the walk, the trot, the canter and the gallop.

In each of these paces the horse's hooves touch the ground in different sequences, and these sequences are called gaits. The manner in which the horse's legs are used is called the action, and this varies between breeds and types.

- Light horses bend their knees less, and the result is a long, smooth stride.
- Ponies tend to pick up their feet in a high action. The ride on a pony tends to be springy.
- Heavy horses, with their straighter shoulders, bend their knees more. This gives them much greater traction and pulling power.

The walk is a four-beat pace during which the horse places its feet on the ground in strides of regular length. Each lateral pair of feet is placed on the ground together. The sequence of footfalls is: near (left) hind, near fore, off (right) hind, off fore.

The walk is generally at about 4.8km/3 miles per hour.

Modern dressage requirements are for four sub-divisions of the walk: the medium, collected, extended, and free.

The trot is a two-beat pace during which the horse places a diagonal pair of feet on the ground together, springs up, and places the other diagonal pair down

with a moment of suspension between each step: thus near hind and off foreleg are down together, then off hind and near forelegs.

Modern dressage requirements are for four sub-divisions of the trot: collected, working, medium, and extended.

Canter is a three beat pace followed by a moment of
suspension when all the hooves are off the ground at the
same time. When circling, the horse should lead with the
inside foreleg and hind leg (this is known as true canter).
When circling left the sequence of the legs are: off hind
leg, followed by right diagonal pair (off fore and near
hind together), then the near foreleg which is the leading
leg. When circling right the sequence is: near hind, near
fore, off hind together (left diagonal pair), off fore (the
leading leg).

A good rider will be able to make his horse change
leading legs in mid-canter (known as a 'flying change').

The gallop, the fastest of the natural gaits, is

generally a four-beat gait. However, there can be variations, depending on the speed.

With the off foreleg leading, the sequence is the near hind leg, then the off hind leg, then near foreleg, then off foreleg. Then all four feet are off the ground together, before the near hindleg touches down again.

The top speed for a gallop is about 69km/43 miles per hour, but the horse cannot maintain this speed for very long.

As well as the four natural gaits, there are some specialized ones.

- The pacing gait is a two-beat movement. The legs move in lateral pairs, that is near fore and near hind followed by off fore and off hind.
- Pacing, which is a faster version of the amble, is a very smooth, comfortable gait.
- Most of the pacing horses come from the Americas. The most famous are the Morgan, the American Saddlebred, and the Missouri Fox Trotter.
- The Peruvian Stepping Horse is a pacing breed from South America.
- The American Standardbred is the fastest pacing horse in the world.
- Some Asian breeds also pace naturally, for example the Kabardin from the northern Caucasus.
- The Icelandic Horse has five gaits – the walk, the trot, the gallop, the pace, or *skeid,* and a unique gait, the *tölt,* which is a four-beat running walk. The animal uses this gait to cross difficult terrain, and it can be very fast indeed.

Anatomy and Movement

The horse is adapted for grazing and running, and its main differences from other mammals stem from these characteristics. It has strong jaws for grinding vegetation, large eyes and good hearing to spot danger, and long strong legs with specialized feet for speed in flight. It has large muscles to cope with its heavy skeleton.

Horses are famous for sleeping standing up. They can do this because of what is known as the 'stay apparatus', an arrangement of tendons and muscles which supports the legs by not allowing the hock to flex or extend without the stifle.

A horse's shape and physical characteristics are called its conformation. Conformation is largely a result of the formation of the skeleton, and the proportion and relationship of one part with another. A well-made horse will have good proportions and a skeleton suitable for the work he is to do. If the proportions – the conformation – are good, he will not only be a better worker, but he will also look pleasing to the eye.

Conformational failings can include an over-long back, weak quarters, sickle hocks, and an insufficient girth.

On level ground, a horse should move with a smooth action, carrying its head straight and evenly with no rolling. Each leg should move cleanly with no interference with the other feet.

Horses are measured in the UK and the USA in 'hands', expressed as 'hands high' (hh). A hand is 10cm/ 4 inches. In Europe, horses are measured in centimetres.

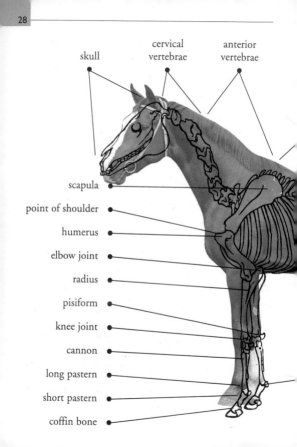

skull

cervical vertebrae

anterior vertebrae

scapula

point of shoulder

humerus

elbow joint

radius

pisiform

knee joint

cannon

long pastern

short pastern

coffin bone

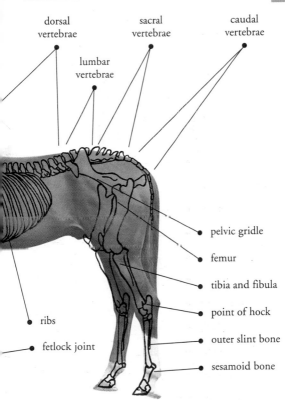

dorsal
vertebrae

lumbar
vertebrae

sacral
vertebrae

caudal
vertebrae

pelvic gridle

femur

tibia and fibula

point of hock

ribs

fetlock joint

outer slint bone

sesamoid bone

Life Cycle of the Horse

Mares reach puberty between about eighteen months and two years of age, although they are not usually ready to give birth until they are about three or four years old. Stallions reach puberty at about a year old, but domestic horses, either kept privately or at stud farms, are not usually put to stud until they are about four.

A mare will come into heat ('season'), that is, be ready to mate, during the summer months every three weeks or so. She will be on heat for about five days at a time, and it is during this period that she will accept a stallion. Her behaviour will change at this time, and she will be restless and edgy.

Different breeds remain capable of breeding until different ages, but the average age at which domestic mares are no longer used for breeding is 15.

A horse's pregnancy lasts eleven months. Just as in humans, the embryo develops during the first months of pregnancy and then grows fast in the final few months.

Four months into a pregnancy the embryo's sex is established, it is recognizably a horse, and its hooves will be formed.

Six months on it is almost 61cm/24 inches long with a full coat of hair.

By eight months it will weigh about 18kg/40lb, and have the beginnings of a mane and tail.

Thereafter growth is rapid until by the 11th month

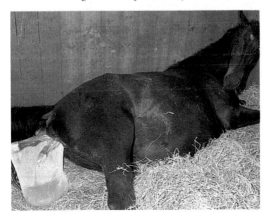

the foal turns itself round ready to be born head and front legs first.

Twin foals are rare, tend to be small and have a poor survival rate.

Most foals are born in early summer, when the weather is kind and feed is abundant. The birth is usually trouble-free, and the mother will carefully lick her foal all over to clean it and to encourage circulation. The foal can stand on its own feet within half-an-hour of birth, and quickly learns to walk and to keep up with its mother, although it will look a little unsteady as its legs have not yet completely straightened out. It has soft feet and a light coat of baby hair, with a short fluffy

mane and tail. It has large eyes in an appealing wide face, and its croup will be noticeably higher than its withers.

By about five weeks the foal's legs have straightened and it will be completely steady on its feet. By six weeks the foal can eat grass, but it will continue to drink its mother's milk until it is about 5-6 months old. This milk is rich in valuable nutrients and will help to protect the foal from infection. In the wild the foal is usually weaned by about six months, but in domestic circumstances weaning often takes place slightly earlier.

By the time the foal is weaned it will have developed a much more adult body shape and proportion,

with its hooves and all its muscles firming up. Its adult coat will have replaced its baby hair.

A foal does not have to wait until its first birthday to be a yearling, as the age of all horses is taken from 1st May of the year in which it is born. Thoroughbreds are the exceptions to this rule: they are deemed to be yearlings on 1st January in the year following their birth.

Yearlings still do not have fully mature bodies. However, bit by bit the withers rise until they are on a level with the croup, giving an adult body shape, and the long bones of the legs harden and strengthen. Most horses are not ready for work much before three years of

age. If a young horse is worked underweight before its leg bones are mature, permanent damage can be caused.In a well-proportioned adult horse the distance between wither and elbow will be approximately the same as the distance between elbow and the ground.

Horses are usually capable of working until at least 20 years of age.

As they grow old, horses fall prey to the same difficulties of old age as any species: circulation and digestion start to fail, teeth wear down and eyesight is less keen. In domestic circumstances it is easier to look after an old horse and to keep its health from failing. In

the wild, once a horse can no longer chew, death is not far away.

Foals are usually born with no teeth although some have two incisors in top and bottom jaw at birth or within days.

By ten days old a foal has cut its two top incisors.

By four to six weeks a foal has cut a further two incisors (laterals) in top and bottom jaws.

By nine to ten months a foal has cut a further two incisors (corners).

The foal will then have a full set of milk teeth.

By five years its milk teeth will have been replaced

with an adult set. It is usual to check the age of a horse by looking at its teeth, which grow longer as it ages, hence the expression 'long in the tooth'.

A horse's teeth also show its age in other ways. Young incisors have grooves, or cup-shaped markings, which wear down over the years.

Adult horses have 24 molars and 12 incisors. Male horses have one additional set of teeth which appear at four years of age; two in the top jaw and two in the lower jaw between incisors and molars.

～ CLASSIFICATION ～

Horse Types

There are certain types which do not have breed status because they lack a fixed character. However, they do have a distinctive 'look'. Such animals often have no pedigree or registration papers, and the breeding may be unknown.

Cob

With the exception of the Welsh Cob, which is a distinct breed, 'cob' refers to any horse between 14 and 15 hh, stocky and strongly built. A cob should be compact and placid, providing a comfortable ride, not too fast, and is ideal for anyone requiring a calm mount. It should be a good strong all-rounder, as comfortable in harness as being ridden. Cobs are traditionally shown with a hogged mane, which shows off its strong sporting look.

Hunter

A horse used for hunting must move freely, gallop on, jump, and have a confident brave character. The type of country in which the hunt takes place is important in the choice of horse. Flat open country with big jumps requires a larger, bolder horse with more Thoroughbred blood: hilly country requires something smaller and more sure-footed. The best hunters are British or Irish-bred, and are often based on a Thoroughbred-Irish Draught cross.

Riding Pony
(SHOW PONY)

The riding pony aims to provide a suitable mount for a child, and can be considered the juvenile equivalent of the Hack. It is usually based on the stalwart Welsh pony, with an outcross to Arab or Thoroughbred to dilute somewhat the strong will of the native pony. The intention is a gentle, good-looking pony with character and a robust constitution.

Hack

The word 'hack' comes from the medieval term 'hackney', meaning a hired horse of poor quality. Gradually it has come to mean a general riding horse, and today's hack is a smallish, good-quality horse with faultless manners and looks, ridden for pleasure. In Europe the popular cross is Thoroughbred and Arab, while in the USA the Saddlebred is favourite.

Racehorse

The racehorse is usually a Thoroughbred, a fleet, highly-strung animal capable of great speed, and often beginning his racing career at the age of three. He is part of a hugely lucrative international industry, in which betting is the central element. It sometimes seems as if a racehorse is reluctant to go in front, and experts suggest that this is because in the wild the herd offers safety from predators. When a jockey uses his whip, the horse thinks it is being attacked and will surge to the front – if he can! Modern racing also includes Quarter Horse racing, trotting, and harness races of all kinds.

Show Jumper

Horses rarely have to jump in the wild unless they are in flight, and their long muzzles make it hard to judge distance. Thus they must trust their rider, and will require his help in the take-off because it will not be possible to see the bar close up. A strong, brave horse is needed, tall enough to tackle obstacles more than 183cm/6 ft high, and with strong quarters.

Polo Pony

The game of polo originated in Persia about 2500 years ago, where it was played by men and women. It is still played in some form or other all over Asia, but the game as it is now played in Britain, the USA, Argentina and India is the game as refined and standardized by the British, who brought it back to England from India in the 19th century. The polo pony is a pony in name only as there is now no restriction on height – the average is now about 15 hh. Argentina dominates the game, so not surprisingly the best polo ponies are bred there. Galloping at up to 64km/40 miles per hour, ponies are encouraged to bump and barge, and a polo pony must be fearless and quite aggressive, very nimble and possessed of great stamina and speed.

HORSE
≈ MANAGEMENT ≈

Learning to Ride

Riding is enormous fun, often allowing a special relationship to develop between you and the horse or pony you ride. It is a relationship based on mutual trust, with rider and mount working together, and is different from that formed with any other animal.

Riding for leisure often provides an opportunity to reach glorious, unspoilt areas of countryside, and to enjoy them once there.

Today anyone can learn to ride, and thousands do!

There are many riding schools throughout the country. It is important to choose a registered school with qualified instructors. Most schools will also offer rides out, usually in groups of up to half a dozen, comprising riders of a similar standard and experience.

A novice rider will be given a gentle, reliable mount experienced with beginners. Schools will lend riders hard hats, to protect the head in case of a fall. Hard hats should be well fitting with a secure fixed harness, they must conform to BSI standard. The most suitable trousers are purpose-made jodhpurs, which are comfortable, close-fitting and hardwearing. Jeans tend to ride up and produce wrinkles which will rub.

Footwear should have smooth soles with heels, and long boots will be the most comfortable. Gloves will keep your hands warm and be comfortable on the reins.

Riding stables usually have a mounting block available. Until a novice develops the knack of mounting, even a pony can seem a long way up! Once in the saddle, the beginner may be led round the schooling ring on a leading rein for a while.

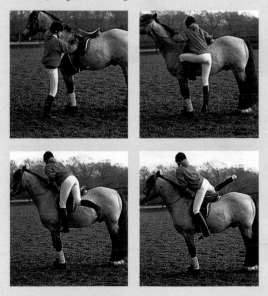

LEARNING TO RIDE: THE BASICS

Walk: Sit in the centre of the saddle, follow the movement of the horse with a supple waist and hips. Allow hands to follow the movement of the horse's head and neck. It is important to look up in order to stay well balanced.

Trot: At the trot the rider may sit or rise. To sit, keep your weight in the saddle all the time. To rise, relax and absorb the bounce through your body, rising a little way out of the saddle for one beat before sitting down gently on the next.

Canter: Relax and keep your weight in the saddle, leaning forwards slightly and moving with the beat of the stride.

Gallop: Grip with your legs, and lean well forwards to help the horse's forward movement. It can help to rise out of the saddle slightly and stand in the stirrups. Stirrups need to be shorter in order to remain over the horse's centre of balance.

Basic Schooling

Successful training aims to produce a fit and supple horse, able and willing to comply with all reasonable requests made of it. Training should adapt the horse's natural resources – strength, speed and sensitivity – to man's requirements. The best results are achieved when the horse's natural qualities are channelled so that it may take pride in its skills.

Schooling is a long, painstaking task, and should operate by a system of reward and punishment, the punishment being the reward withheld.

A foal should be handled frequently and gently from its first days to encourage trust in humans, and to learn what is acceptable behaviour. During its first week it can have a light halter put regularly on and off, and be led beside its mother.

By the age of three, the young horse should know how to behave when handled, tied up, groomed, and led. Now it should have a few days during which it is loose in a lunge ring for half an hour per day, getting used to being in a confined space.

The lunge ring is an indoor or outdoor paddock large enough for the young horse to be walked round in a circle at the end of the lunge rein, which is usually about 7m/8 yards long. The horse wears a lunge cavesson (which is a well padded and well fitted headcollar with swivel rings on the noseband), and the trainer will carry a whip (used to guide, not to beat, the horse).

The horse can start to become accustomed to a comfortable rubber snaffle bit and a light saddle with no stirrups. Boots are a good idea as the horse can catch its feet before it learns a good gait.

For two or three lessons the horse will walk only, learning to accept gentle control and the discipline necessary before being ridden.

The horse will then learn to trot on the lunge rein, the trot being the main gait of the lunge lesson. Once able to trot calmly and with control, the horse moves on to canter.

Next comes learning to accept the weight of a person, and this process is called 'backing'.

From now on, the young horse's lessons will alternate unmounted lunge work with more active ridden work and leading out on a long rein.

Lungeing helps the horse to acquire a free forward movement and promotes the correct development of muscles and joints; later, sensitive ridden work helps to increase strength and balance. The horse will learn to work with a good extension and stretch, and will wish to please its rider, and to perform without stress or discomfort.

Buying a Horse

Before you consider buying a horse or pony, the very first thing to think about is where you will be keeping it. You must have adequate shelter and grazing: a pony kept outside to grass must have at least 0.8 hectares/2 acres.

Remember that owning a horse will take up a great deal of time. Remember too that horses are expensive to buy, and that you will also need to pay for tack and equipment, food, insurance, the vet, and the farrier.

Then you must decide what kind of horse you would like to buy. It must be suitable for your purpose: you must consider your own size and weight, what type of riding you wish to do, and the facilities at your disposal. For instance, if your horse will be kept outside, it will be a good idea to buy a hardy breed!

Buying a horse at auction is best left to the professionals as you will have only a short time to try the animals. Equestrian magazines carry advertisements of horses for sale, or you can contact a reputable horse dealer, who may have several animals which you could look at.

Ride any horse you are interested in. Ask questions about it – find out about its behaviour in traffic, when travelling, when it is being shod. In particular, check the following:

- nose: – nostrils should be free from any discharge.
- eyes: – should be clear, with smooth eyelids
- teeth: – front teeth should be level, with no damage or uneven wear

- feet: – should have no cracks, and hooves should be symmetrical
- legs: – tendons should be hard with no puffiness, soreness or heat, and there should be no lameness
- Coat: – should be shiny and clean with no blemishes, swellings or parasites

Always insist on a vet's inspection. If possible, get the horse on a one- or two-week trial. Obtain a warranty from the seller covering all the points in which you are interested.

Lastly, once you have found your horse and agreed a price, remember that the purchaser pays carriage and the cost of the vet certificate!

Nutrition and Feeding

Wild horses in their natural habitat eat only grass and perhaps plants such as dandelions, grazing and moving slowly across the land. Since they have been domesticated, the size of horses and their capacity for work has increased and with it their requirements for more and better food.

The nutrition of horses is a specialized subject under continual research, but all agree that, along with roughage and water, horses require various nutrients:

- proteins
- fats/carbohydrates
- minerals
- vitamins (A, B, C, D)

Every individual horse has its own requirements for the amount of food it needs daily, depending on weight, work load, climate and the horse's own constitution, but the average would be between two and three per cent of its bodyweight, with pregnant mares, growing foals and working horses requiring slightly more.

A horse may be given the following types of foods:

- fodder, such as hay, lucerne or silage
- concentrates (cereal concentrates such as oats, or non-cereal concentrates such as pony nuts)
- other foods include barley, bran, linseed, sugar beet, molasses, carrots, apples
- mineral and vitamin supplements, especially if required to correct a particular problem
- salt

Give your horse only fresh, good-quality food. Horses have quite delicate constitutions, and the fungal spores in mouldy hay can trigger an allergic response and other difficulties. They can also be fussy about their water, which will often remain undrunk if it is stale or lying in a dirty container. Horses require between 22 and 90 litres/5 and 20 gallons of water a day, as up to 50 per cent of its bodyweight is made up of water, which is vital to regulate body temperature, to maintain the health of cells, and to aid digestion and the metabolism. It is also a vital constituent of saliva, sweat and urine.

Horses are creatures of habit and like to be fed at regular times. They have comparatively small stomachs, with a capacity of only about 8-15 litres/2-3 gallons, and so it is better to give a horse three small feeds a day than two large ones.

Do not feed a horse immediately before or after exercise: a full stomach presses on the lungs, reducing the horse's effectiveness, and after exercise the digestion will not be working to full capacity.

Changes in your horse's diet should be introduced very gradually, not only to accustom it to the new food but also to allow the microbial population in the gut to adapt.

A healthy horse will have a good appetite. It must have good, even teeth so that chewing causes no discomfort, and parasites in the gut must be kept down with special supplements so that nutrients are not lost.

An old horse will probably require more food and perhaps special supplements to keep it healthy.

Don't forget that certain plants are poisonous to horses! These include ragwort, foxglove and bracken, but you should ask your local vet for details of others in your area.

Grooming

An animal's outer skin (the 'epidermis') provides protection and warmth. The inner skin (the 'dermis') contains hair roots, sweat and oil glands, blood vessels and nerves. Sweating regulates body temperature and also throws out some body wastes. A hardworking domestic horse, eating more heat-producing food than a wild horse, sweats more too, so it is important to keep his skin clear of sweat residue and scurf which might cause skin diseases if left. The muscles of a working horse benefit from the massage too.

The end result of this important cleaning process is the one we notice – appearance.

Tools:

- hoof pick – a blunt hook to pick dirt and stones out of the hoofs
- dandy brush – stiff fibre brush to clean off dried mud
- body brush and curry comb (used together) – body brush cleans off scurf and curry comb cleans out the body brush
- sponge – for the face, separate sponge for the dock
- sweat scraper – a curved rubber strip to scrape off sweat lather
- wisp – a twisted rope of straw used for massage
- stable rubber – a finishing cloth to provide gloss

Your horse should be given a light grooming once-over ('quartering') before exercise and should be well dried after exercise ('cooling and drying off').

The main grooming of the day, 'strapping', is a vigorous and thorough operation. Start with the hoof pick and check all the feet. With the dandy brush remove all the dried mud (horses are not usually washed in the UK unless the weather is very warm). Then with the body brush, brush the horse all over. It is customary to start on the horse's near-side, working from the neck along the body, then doing the legs. Do the other side next. Then sponge down the horse's face and dock. Lastly attend to the mane and tail (the mane should lie on the horse's off-side).

CLIPPING

Hardy native ponies living out seldom sweat as they take no more exercise than they wish, and they need their shaggy, greasy coats as protection and for warmth. For working horses, a thick coat is a positive disadvantage, and most are clipped in the winter, once in October or November and then again early in the year. A rug should be provided as a substitute when the horse is not exercising.

There are five types of clip: full trace clip, small trace clip, blanket clip, full clip, hunter clip.

To prepare a horse for a show there are various finishing touches you can provide:

- mane and tail can be plaited
- hooves can be oiled
- the coat can be back-combed through a template to create patterns – the chequerboard on the hindquarters is especially popular.

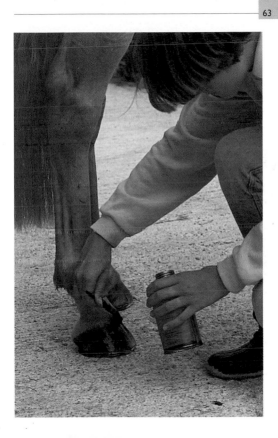

Saddlery

A horse's tack – his saddle, bridle, or harness – can be one of your biggest expenses, but it is not worth buying cheaply as poor quality tack will not last, and may not be comfortable in use.

SADDLES

Saddles are for the comfort of both rider and horse, as they distribute the rider's weight evenly over the strong muscles of the horse's back. Correct fit is very important.

The first saddles, in use about 2000 years ago, were padded wooden frames, and the basic idea has not changed. Today there are specialist saddles for different types of use. The general purpose saddle is probably the most useful for, as its name implies, all kinds of general riding. It is constructed of leather, well padded, on a beechwood frame called the 'tree'.

Other types of saddle are:
- for racing – very light, sometimes no more than 225g /8 oz
- for jumping – constructed to throw the weight forward slightly
- for dressage – with long flaps and long girth straps. British and Continental dressage saddles differ slightly
- for eventing
- for showing
- for polo – very strongly constructed
- Western saddles – broad and comfortable, with high cantle, and strong tree at the front to tie lariat to

The girth fastens the saddle on to the horse's back. It can be made of leather, webbing, nylon, or string (multiple strands of man-made fibre). Webbing is very good, as it is absorbent and can be cleaned easily.

A numnah is a saddle-shaped pad worn under the saddle to prevent pressure sores. It can be made from many materials including a thin felt pad, quilted cotton or sheepskin.

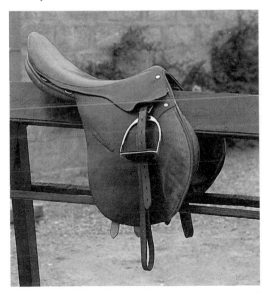

BRIDLES

The bridle, constructed of a headpiece and reins, holds the bit in the horse's mouth. It is usually made of leather, with the parts buckled together to facilitate repair. A bridle is for one bit, for two bits, or none.

- Snaffle – the simplest bit, with either a jointed or a straight mouthpiece, applying pressure to the corners of the horse's mouth.

- Double bridle – more sophisticated, with two bits, called a bridoon and a curb. For use with a well-schooled horse.
- Pelham – halfway between a snaffle and a double bridle.
- Gag – applies an upward sliding pull.
- Hackamore – a bitless bridle.

Bits are usually made of stainless steel.

Reins are usually made of leather for showing, but for general purpose use rubber-covered leather is harder-wearing. Plaited leather or cotton are also comfortable and strong, but can stretch.

All tack should be kept clean and supple. Leather should be washed and dried, then treated with saddle soap or neatsfoot oil. Stainless steel should be washed and dried. Anything man-made can be washed in the ordinary way.

❧ PONIES ❧

Introduction

Around 6000 years ago, just before horses were first domesticated, it is thought that two separate types of pony evolved on the plains and steppes of Eurasia. Type 1, as it is called, continued its development in north-west Europe, probably from Tarpan stock. It was a tough, waterproof little animal, and its descendants include the Exmoor pony and the Icelandic pony. Type 2 was larger. It evolved in northern Eurasia, probably from the Asiatic Wild Horse. However, we know that the Asiatic Wild Horse has 66 chromosomes, the genetic material which passes characteristics from generation to generation, whereas Type 2 has 64, as does the modern horse.

Although ponies share a common ancestry with horses, they are different from them in several important ways. They stand below 15 hh (150cm), and have different proportions, being shorter-legged in relation to their height. Their body length is greater than their height at the withers, and the length of the head equals the shoulder length.

Ponies tend to have longer manes and tails, and shaggier coats, and they are generally constitutionally stronger and longer-lived. They have a rather different action, and are surer-footed, with hard little feet which often do not require shoeing.

In addition, ponies are often of a more independent cast of mind, and can be possessed of powerful native cunning.

Not every country of the world has an indigenous pony population, but today ponies are so popular that the better known breeds are exported all over the world to feed an ever-growing business in leisure riding for children.

Ponies in History

Tougher and stronger for their size than horses, ponies have always been the popular choice for transport of all kinds. They are cheap to feed and easy to keep, too, and are usually dogged and brave. Especially in mountainous regions, ponies are valued for agricultural work and transport of all kinds, from drawing passenger carts to carrying contraband across high mountain passes.

The Vikings took their ponies with them on their open longboats, relying on them for meat and milk as well as for transport on land. They also liked to arrange savage fights between stallions, often to the death, with the winner much prized at stud thereafter. Celtic traders also rode ponies, often accompanied by a pack pony burdened down with goods.

Later, as the Romans spread through the known world, ponies went with them. Although the Roman Empire was founded on the fighting strength of its infantrymen, supplies of all kinds were nevertheless transported by ponies, and many vassal states provided cavalry units, mostly riding their native ponies. In this way ponies brought to Britain by the Romans made their way to west Wales and as far north as Hadrian's Wall, where their successors live today.

Beyond the Wall, the Scots favoured their hardy native Highland Ponies. During the Jacobite Rebellion in 1715 the clansmen, mounted on Highland Ponies, were, however, no match for the English with their superior numbers and firepower.

The ferocious Genghis Khan swept into Europe in the 12th century, he and his hordes were mounted on fearless Mongolian ponies. The Mongol hordes valued their ponies highly and took meticulously good care of them, relying upon them for many essentials, from skins to wear, to dung to burn on their fires.

In China, 1300 years before Christ, ponies were already in use to draw sophisticated wheeled vehicles, both harness and vehicle being far in advance of anything found in the West. The Chinese were enormously inventive and practical, and are responsible for nearly all the advances made to harness: they

invented the harness strap which passes round the lower quarters, enabling the horse to brake a load, and also the breast strap and horse collar, which provide far greater traction for the horse.

America's legendary Pony Express was inaugurated in 1860 and lasted for only two years, before being overtaken by the invention of the telegraph. Its starting point was in Missouri, and the 3163km/1966 mile route to California was covered in ten days by teams of riders, each man riding 96.5km/60 miles. There were 190 relay stations, 400 ponies and 100 young riders.

Pit Ponies

Coal fuelled Britain's Industrial Revolution in the 19th century, enabling not only the massive increase in factory mechanization but also the fast, cheap transport of goods. Although coal had been surface-mined in quite a small way for centuries, it was only now that deep mining became possible.

Men, women and small children laboured down mines in atrocious conditions all over Britain, until in 1847 women and children were prohibited by Act of Parliament from working underground. Thousands of Shetland ponies were drafted in to help fill the gaps left by the departure of half the workforce. They worked and were stabled underground for up to the 20 years of their working life. Their main task was to haul wagons from the coalface to the surface or to the hoist. Other ponies worked at the pit head, turning the windlass of the hoist.

The last pit ponies retired in 1994 from the Ellington Colliery in Northumberland.

Falabella

Use: Miniature carriage horse, pet, not ridden.
Height: Up to 7 hh. **Colours:** All solid and part
colours, with Appaloosa especially popular.
Identifying features: Heads can be large, but
proportions are usually those of a horse; flat withers,
upright shoulders, fine legs and feet.

The Falabella is the smallest horse in the world. It was
developed by the Falabella family at their ranch near
Buenos Aires in Argentina, using the smallest of Shetlands
crossed with Thoroughbreds. They then bred for size,
taking care not to fix the kind of conformational
weakness that can come with in-breeding. Falabellas are
strong for their height, gentle and hardy.

Galiceno

Use: Saddle, harness. **Height:** 12–14 hh.
Colours: All solid colours. **Identifying features:** Neat
head on slender neck, upright shoulders, narrow
compact body, short back, slim legs, small feet.

The Galiceno of Mexico is actually a small horse which takes its name from Galicia in northern Spain. Its ancestors, ultimately descended from the Iberian Sorraia and Garranos, were brought to the Americas by early Spanish settlers. It has been recognized as a breed since 1958, and is now popular throughout the USA for many different uses. Galicenos are tough, intelligent and responsive.

Sable Island

Use: Feral, saddle. **Height:** 14–15 hh.
Colours: Most solid colours. **Identifying features:** Large
head, narrow body, light legs, shaggy coat.

Sable Island is a barren, windswept island off the coast of Nova Scotia, but for the last 400 years or so some 50 herds of wild horses have survived there. They may be descended from Norman horses abandoned by early settlers, but today are poor in conformation despite their obvious hardihood. They can be trained to the saddle if caught young enough.

Pony of the Americas

Use: Saddle. **Height:** 11.2–13.2 hh.
Colours: Appaloosa colours and patterns.
Identifying features: Neat head with mottled skin on muzzle, good shoulders and deep chest, short back, rounded body, short good legs, strong hindquarters.

In 1954 Mr Leslie Boomhower of Mason City, Iowa, crossed a Shetland stallion with an Appaloosa mare. The result was a small pony with Appaloosa marking which Mr Boomhower called Black Hand. Later there were outcrosses to Arab and Quarter Horses, and the breed standard calls for a pony with the appearance of a miniature Quarter Horse-Arab cross. This, the first pony to have been developed in the USA, is gentle and intelligent, and makes an ideal child's pony.

Chincoteague and Assateague

Use: Feral; some saddle. **Height:** as hh.
Colours: All colours. **Identifying features:** Plain head,
short round body, weak legs with poor joints,
shaggy winter coat.

Two kinds of pony, very much alike, live wild on the small islands of Chincoteague and Assateague off the eastern coast of the USA. There are only about 200 ponies in all, probably descended from early settlers' stock which was lost or abandoned. The herds have only been widely known since around the 1920s, since when they have been outcrossed with Shetlands, Welsh Ponies and Pintos. They remain feral, and are considered stubborn and uncompromising.

American Shetland

Use: Showing, racing, harness driving. **Height:** Up to 11.2 hh. **Colours:** All solid colours. **Identifying features:** Long head with straight profile, prominent withers, long narrow body, long slim legs, long mane and tail, short coat unlike Shetland ancestors.

The American Shetland is a man-made variant of the original Scottish pony. The first Shetlands arrived in the USA in 1885, and within 50 years the breed had been crossed with Hackney ponies to produce a lighter, taller pony, more refined in shape and with a good action. The American Shetland is not as tough as its ancestors, but is strong for its size and very versatile.

Dülmen

Use: Feral. **Height:** 12.3 hh. **Colours:** Dun, black, brown. **Identifying features:** Plain head on short neck, strong compact body, short legs.

The Dülmen is found in the Westphalia region of Germany, and is that country's only existing native pony; the Senner, once found in the Teutoburger Wald, is now extinct. The last existing herd of about 100 Dülmens runs wild on the Duke of Croÿ's estates at Mierfelder Bruch. They are of mixed origin and have themselves contributed to the development of the early Hanoverian horses.

Shetland

Use: Harness, saddle. **Height:** 26–42inches (Shetlands are not measured in hands). **Colours:** All colours. **Identifying features:** Small head on sloping shoulders, deep thick-set body, short back, short legs with some feathering, tough feet.

The Shetland pony is one of the world's most popular ponies, and a favourite first mount for a child. It is one of nine surviving native British breeds of pony, and has lived in the Shetland and Orkney Islands, off the north coast of Scotland, for 2000 years. It is exceptionally strong for its size, and is tough enough to survive the harsh conditions of its homeland. In the winter the Shetland grows an abundant, warm coat, and when food is scarce it will even eat seaweed. Shetlands have a free action and are highly intelligent: they can, however, be strong-willed and even bad-tempered.

Highland

Use: Saddle, pack, harness. **Height:** 14.2 hh.
Colours: All colours, including dun with dorsal stripe.
Identifying features: Small head on muscular neck,
solid deep body, short strong legs with some
feathering, good feet.

The largest and strongest of Britain's native breeds, the Highland pony was once found in two strains: the mainland Garron (up to 14.2 hh) and the smaller Western Islands strain. Today there is no official distinction between the two. In the 16th century French and Spanish horses were used to interbreed. The Highland pony is the utility pony of the Scottish highlands, sure-footed and robust but also sensitive and intelligent. Because it is so strong, it is in demand for all kinds of use, from trekking to pack work.

Dales

Use: Riding, trekking, farm work. **Height:** 13.2–14.2 hh.
Colours: Black; sometimes dark bay or dark brown.
Identifying features: Neat head on strong neck, deep
strong shoulders, short back, deep girth, short legs with
some feathering, thick mane and tail, short flat
cannons, good feet.

This large, strong pony comes from north-east
England and probably descends from Friesians
brought to Britain by the Romans 2000 years ago. In the
18th century Dales ponies were developed as pack ponies
taking lead ore from the mines of Allendale and Alston
Moor to the eastern seaports of England. A century later,
outcrosses were made to Welsh Cobs and Clydesdales, but
recently the Clydesdale influence has diminished, leaving
a sturdy pony with great stamina and a calm temperament.

Fell

Use: Saddle, harness. **Height:** 13–14 hh. **Colours:**
Black, brown, bay; sometimes grey. **Identifying features:**
Small head on long neck, sloping shoulders, compact
muscular body, strongly muscled quarters, strong legs
with feathering, long thick mane and tail, hard feet.

The Fell pony is a close relative of the Dales pony,
arising from west of the Pennines in the north of
England, but is smaller, lighter and can be preferred for
riding. It is immensely strong, and has been used for
carting and farm work as well as riding. It is descended
from Friesians brought to England by the Romans, and
also from the now-extinct Scottish Galloway pony. Today
it is popular for riding and as a trotter.

Tibetan Pony or Nanfan

Use: Pack, saddle, harness. **Height:** 12 hh.
Colours: All. **Identifying features:** Small tough frame
with short hard legs.

The Tibetan pony is a good worker, intelligent, and
capable of carrying large loads over great distances
without complaint. It is descended from the Mongolian
horse which stamped its character on so many of the
mountain ponies of the area.

Dartmoor

Use: Saddle. **Height:** 12.2 hh. **Colours:** Bay, brown, black. **Identifying features:** Small head with small ears, strong neck, shoulders set back, strong quarters, slim hard legs with short cannons and flat joints, full mane and tail, good hard feet.

Small, hardy wild ponies have roamed free on Dartmoor, in south-west England, for at least 1000 years. From the 12th to the 15th centuries they were used to carry tin from the local tin mines, and they have also been used for some agricultural work. Since then, numerous outcrosses have produced a good riding pony with an exceptionally smooth action (because the Dartmoor pony does not lift its knees very high while moving). Nimble and resourceful, the Dartmoor makes an ideal riding pony.

Exmoor

Use: Riding, cross-breeding. **Height:** 12.2–12.3 hh.
Colours: Bay, brown or dun with mealy muzzle; no
white' **Identifying features:** Small head, thick neck,
deep chest, short legs with good bone, neat hard feet.
Eyes are hooded ('toad eyes'), coat is almost double-
textured and the tail has a fan-like growth at the top
('ice tail'), for protection against the elements; Exmoors
have a seventh molar not present in other breeds.

The Exmoor is the oldest native British breed. Its
ancestors are unknown, but probably made the
journey to Britain before it became an island. The
Exmoor has changed little over the centuries, perhaps
because of its geographical isolation in the far south-
western tip of England. It is famously hardy and nimble,
and makes a good child's pony despite its independent
nature. Once a year all the Exmoors are rounded
up and branded.

New Forest Pony

Use: Saddle, harness. **Height:** 12–14.2 hh. **Colours:** All except piebald or skewbald. **Identifying features:** Large head, short back with full girth, sloping shoulders, muscular quarters, good feet and legs.

The New Forest, in south England, once extended as far as Dartmoor, and the ponies of these areas probably intermingled. Today New Forest ponies still run wild, but because they are less isolated the type is less fixed. Indeed, New Forest ponies come into daily contact with humans, and are calm and friendly when trained. Improvements to the stock using Welsh, Arab and Thoroughbred were tried without great success, and since 1938 there has been no new blood. Despite some weaknesses in conformation, they are surefooted and make good riding ponies. Auctions of New Forest ponies are held once a year. People who live within the forest and who hold Rights of Common Pasturage are known as Commoners and are allowed to run their ponies in the forest.

Welsh Ponies

Welsh ponies, considered by many to be the prettiest of the British native ponies, have been running wild in Wales for centuries. Julius Caesar is even said to have founded a stud for them in Wales, and to have introduced Oriental blood. In the 19th century, Thoroughbred, Barb and Arab blood was introduced, and the result is a line of ponies with distinctively fine appearance and movement. Since 1902 there have been four sections to the Welsh Pony and Cob Stud Book.

Welsh Mountain Pony

Use: Riding **Height:** 12 hh. **Colours:** Usually grey; also all other colours except piebald and skewbald **Identifying features:** Small head with concave face, crested neck, sloping shoulders, short back with deep girth, slender legs with short cannons, flat joints and good bone, neat feet, high-set tail.

This is the base for the other three types, and is the most common of all the British mountain and moorland breeds. As well the elegance it shares with its cousins, it has retained all its native hardiness and soundness.

Welsh Pony

Use: Riding. **Height:** 13.2 hh. **Colours:** All colours except piebald and skewbald. **Identifying features:** Similar to Welsh Mountain Pony, but taller and more lightly built, with exceptionally good proportions.

Originally the result of crossings between Welsh Mountain Ponies and Welsh Cobs, the modern pony is founded on three stallions of Arab-Barb descent. The Welsh pony is graceful and has a good action, lower and smoother than that of the Welsh Mountain Pony. It is more versatile than the Mountain Pony because of its size. The Welsh Pony is predominently a riding pony.

Welsh Pony of Cob Type

> **Use:** Riding. harness **Height:** 13.2 hh.
> **Colours:** Any solid. **Identifying features:** Good head on strong shoulders, deep powerful back, good girth, short muscular legs, high knee action.

Sections C and D are for the Cob types of Welsh Pony. The Section C pony is the smaller of the two. Once extensively used as a farm animal, today it is popular for riding and trekking. It shares its cousins' characteristics of robustness and durability. The Cob Type was usually considered to be a farm pony, working on the Welsh hill farms and slate mines until after the Second World War when, nearing extinction, a new Section (C) was opened in the stud book to preserve it.

Welsh Cob

> **Use:** Riding, harness. **Height:** 15 hh. **Colours:** Any solid. **Identifying features:** Good head on strong shoulders, deep powerful back, good girth, short muscular legs with some feathering, high knee action.

The Welsh Cob, at up to 15 hh, could be called a horse. It looks like a larger version of the Welsh Mountain pony, and makes a versatile mount, with an easy action and a natural jumping ability. It is also good in harness and very strong.

Landais

Use: Riding. **Height:** 11.3–13.1 hh
Colours: Bay, brown, chestnut, black. **Identifying features:** Neat head on thickset neck, prominent withers, straight back, well-muscled legs with good bone, thick mane and tail, tail high-set.

One of three pony breeds native to France, the Landais comes from the Lande region of south-west France. It is descended from primitive local stock, improved by outcrossings to Arabs in the 19th century. After the Second World War numbers were so low that new blood was again needed, and further outcrossings to Arab and to Welsh Section B stock were made. The Landais has a good temperament and action, and is widely used by children in France since the establishment of Pony Clubs there in the 1970s.

Connemara

> **Use:** Saddle. **Height:** 13–14.2 hh.
> **Colours:** Usually grey; also black, brown, dun, bay.
> **Identifying features:** Good head, well carried on
> medium-length neck, sloping shoulders, deep compact
> body, strong legs with good bone.

The Connemara is Ireland's only indigenous pony, and is named for the county of Connemara in the far west of Ireland. Its ancestors include the small Celtic pony, and later Spanish horses brought by traders – and perhaps also Spanish horses saved from shipwrecks following the Spanish Armada in 1588. Outcrosses to Welsh ponies and Thoroughbred have improved the breed, which is popular today all over Europe as a good jumper, fast and large enough to be ridden by adults. It remains a frugal, sensible pony.

Bashkir

Use: Pack, draught, milk, meat. **Height:** 14 hh.
Colours: Chestnut, bay, dun.
Identifying features: Heavy head on thick neck, flat
back with low withers and upright shoulders,
wide back and good girth, short legs,
hard feet (usually unshod).

The Bashkir evolved in the southern foothills of the
Ural mountains of Russia in prehistoric times,
probably based on the primitive Tarpan. Breeding centres
have been established in the area since the 19th century,
producing these durable, patient ponies capable of work
under any climatic conditions existing on the most
frugal of diets.

Zemaituka

Use: Saddle, pack. **Height:** 13–14 hh.
Colours: Usually dun with dorsal stripe.
Identifying features: Thickset head and body, short
strong legs, thick shaggy coat.

The Zemaituka lives under extremes of
temperature and with only poor fodder in the
northernmost areas of Russia. It is descended from the
Asiatic Wild Horse, and may have some Oriental blood.
It is enormously rugged and strong.

Ariègeois

Use: Riding, harness. **Height:** 13.1–14.3 hh.
Colours: Black. **Identifying features:** Light head on upright neck and shoulders, flat withers, long back, short legs with poor conformation and some feather, hard feet, coarse thick mane and tail, thick growth of hair on lower jaw in winter.

This mountain pony from the eastern Pyrenees is also known as the Cheval de Mérens. It is of ancient descent – there are wall paintings of horses in the area some 30,000 years old – and has been influenced by Roman pack horses, Oriental horses and Barbs. The Ariègeois is very hardy and surefooted, and copes well on rough mountain tracks. A stud book was opened in 1947. The Ariègeois is still used for agricultural work in inaccessible areas of the mountains as well as for a riding pony.

Bardigiano

Use: Light draught, pack. **Height:** 12–13 hh. **Colours:** All solid colours. **Identifying features:** Small head with short ears, arched neck on strong upright shoulders, powerful compact body with deep girth, short strong legs with good joints and bone, long mane and tail.

This mountain pony from northern Italy is little known outside its home, yet it is attractive and strong. It is related to the Avelignese and the Haflinger, and shows in its conformation the Oriental influence of El Bedavi, the Arab stallion that was also the founder of the Haflinger. The Bardigiano is robust and sure-footed as befits a working mountain pony.

Gotland

Use: Saddle, harness. **Height:** 12–12.2 hh. **Colours:** All colours. **Identifying features:** Small head, short neck, long back, sloping quarters, narrow frame, short legs, low-set tail, hard feet.

The Gotland pony is Scandinavia's oldest pony breed, and has lived wild on the Swedish island of Gotland for centuries. Descended from the Tarpan, it is thought to have some Arab blood too, and resembles the Huçul and Konik of Poland. Once a good utility farm horse, today it is favoured as a riding pony and is known for its gentle nature.

Icelandic

> **Use:** Transport, farming, racing, meat.
> **Height:** 12.3–13.2 hh. **Colours:** All colours.
> **Identifying features:** Heavy head, thick in the jowl,
> strong short neck, compact powerful body, upright shoulders,
> short strong legs with short cannons and sound feet.

When the Vikings sailed to the cold, volcanic island of Iceland sometime after AD 860, they took with them in their open boats a stock of tough ponies from their northern lands. An attempt to improve the stock with Oriental blood failed, and in 930 the Icelandic parliament forbade the introduction of any further new blood: and there has been none since. The Icelanders care deeply for their independent little horses – as they are always called – and respect their assertive nature.

Skyros

> Use: Saddle, harness, pack. **Height:** 9.1–11 hh.
> **Colours:** Bay, dun. **Identifying features:** Small neat
> head, narrow body and quarters, straight shoulders,
> tendency to cow hocks, small feet, black in colour.

The tough little Skyrian Horse, as Skyrian breeders call
it, has lived wild on the mountainous Greek island of
Skyros since antiquity. It has been used as a pack and
general utility animal for centuries, and is perhaps descended
from the Tarpan and Horse Type 4. It is willing and agile.

Fjord

> Use: Pack, harness, saddle. **Height:** 13–14 hh.
> **Colours:** Dun. **Identifying features:** Small head on
> thick neck merging without definition into shoulders,
> broad chest, heavy shoulders, flat withers, powerful
> rounded body, short legs with some feathering.

Norway's Fjord pony still looks strikingly like its
ancestor, the Asiatic Wild Horse, with its dun
colour, dorsal stripe, and upright mane. Paintings and
carvings of horses looking like this and dating back to
Viking times can be found in many sites in Norway. The
Fjord pony is popular throughout Europe as their stamina
and courage make them ideal for harness work of all types
as well as for riding.

Haflinger

Use: Riding, draught, harness, forestry.
Height: 13–14 hh. **Colours:** Palomino or chestnut with flaxen mane and tail. **Identifying features:** Good head on arched neck, well-made shoulders, good girth, good feet, excellent, strong legs with short cannons.

The Haflinger is the sturdy mountain pony of the Austrian Tirol, with its principal stud today in Jenesien. It is descended from local ponies and extinct Alpine Heavy Horses, and is thus technically a coldblood. However, the breed was outcrossed to the Arab stallion El Bedavi XXII, and the result is a very good pony with a fixed type. It is not usually worked until the age of four, and it said to be able to continue to work until the age of about 40.

Caspian Pony

Use: Saddle, harness. **Height:** 10–12 hh.
Colours: Bay, brown, chestnut, grey. **Identifying features:** Arab-type head on long neck, well-sloped shoulders (giving fast, low stride), narrow body with short back, strong quarters, fine legs with long cannons, tail set and carried high.

The Caspian Pony, actually a miniature horse, may be the direct descendant of the miniature Mesopotamian horse of antiquity, known as Horse Type 4. Once thought to be extinct, it was rediscovered on the shores of the Caspian Sea in Iran in 1965 by an American traveller, Mrs Louise L. Firouz, and is now bred in the UK, Australia, New Zealand, and the USA as well as at Norouzabad in Iran. It is spirited yet gentle, with an excellent smooth action, and is often used unshod.

Sorraia

Use: Harness. **Height:** 12.2–13 hh. **Colours:** Grey-dun usually with black mane and tail. **Identifying features:** Short head with black-tipped ears, strong neck, deep compact body, short legs, low-set tail.

This hardy, vigorous pony native to the area round the rivers Sor and Raia running through Spain and Portugal may be one of the earliest breeds to be domesticated in Europe. Probably descended from the Tarpan, it was later influenced by Barb blood from north Africa, and must itself have contributed to the celebrated Spanish Horse. Once a useful farm worker, today its numbers are depleted.

Bosnian

Use: Harness, pack. **Height:** 13–14.2 hh. **Colours:** Dun, brown, chestnut, black, grey. **Identifying features:** Large head on short strong neck, low withers, upright shoulders, broad body with deep girth, strong legs and feet.

The Bosnian pony is very similar in type to the Polish Huçul, and is also directly descended from the ancient Tarpan. The Bosnian pony is widely used on farms throughout the Balkan region and in former Yugoslavia.

Huçul

Use: Harness, pack. **Height:** 12.1–13 hh.
Colours: Dun, bay, piebald, skewbald.
Identifying features: Short blunt head, short neck, flat withers and upright shoulders, compact body, short legs, sound feet, high-set tail, coat tends to shaggy.

The Huçul is a native of the Carpathian Mountains of Poland, and descends directly from the 'primitive' Tarpan with perhaps some Asiatic Wild Horse and Oriental blood mixed in. The breed has been improved in recent years, and is still a strong working horse on the remote farms of Poland, renowned for carrying heavy loads.

Konik

> **Use:** Light draught, harness. **Height:** 12–13 hh.
> **Colours:** Usually dun with dorsal stripe.
> **Identifying features:** Large head on short strong neck,
> low withers, upright shoulders, broad body with deep
> girth, strong legs and feet.

The Polish word Konik means 'small horse', and this close relative to the Huçul does still bear a distinct resemblance to the ancient Tarpan. The Konik, willing and docile, is the utility horse of the lowland farms of Poland. Today it is bred at the Polish state stud, and by many small farmers.

Basuto

> **Use:** Saddle. **Height:** 14.2 hh.
> **Colours:** Chestnut, brown, bay, grey. **Identifying
> features:** Neat head on long neck, straight shoulders,
> long back, short legs, hard feet.

The Basuto is not native to Basutoland in Africa, but is the descendant of the Cape Horse, which is itself the result of crossing Arab, Barb, and Thoroughbred stock, taken to Cape Province in South Africa by early European settlers. The Basuto diminished in size in the fierce climate, and is today an extremely hardy, brave pony used for trekking and, sometimes, for polo.

Sumba

Use: Saddle, pack. **Height:** 12.2 hh. **Colours:** Dun with dorsal stripe. **Identifying features:** Small head on very short neck, small body, very strong back and legs.

Indonesia, a chain of some 300 islands, supports several sorts of small pony. They all derive ultimately from the primitive Mongolian horse, and were imported to the islands many centuries ago. The Sumba is identical to the Sumbawa, although they live separately on the two islands from which they take their names. They are exceptionally strong, and able, despite their small size, to carry adult men and large loads.

Timor

> **Use:** Saddle, harness. **Height:** 11–12 hh.
> **Colours:** Usually dark, sometimes cream mane and tail.
> **Identifying features:** Small head and short neck,
> straight slight body, tail high-set, bushy mane and tail.

The Timor is the smallest of the Indonesian native ponies. It was probably introduced by the Portuguese, (whose colony Timor was), from India, and then in turn imported to Australia from 1803. The Indonesians found these little ponies much to their liking and used them everywhere to ride, and as work horses. They are famous for their commonsense and powers of endurance.

Java

> **Use:** Harness, saddle. **Height:** 12.2 hh.
> **Colours:** All colours. **Identifying features:** Small head,
> slight build, light legs.

The durable Java pony is slightly larger than the other Indonesian breeds, and has adapted well to hard work in an extreme climate. Barb and Arab blood have helped to raise the standard of conformation of these ponies, which despite their scrawny appearance are capable of pulling fully-laden taxi carts through the streets of Javanese towns.

Padang

Use: Harness, saddle. **Height:** 12.2 hh.
Colours: All colours. **Identifying features:** Small head,
slight build, light legs.

The Padang of Sumatra was developed by the Dutch at Padang Mengabes from the Batak pony, using Arab blood to improve conformation and action. The result is a lightly-built pony, like all the Indonesian breeds far stronger than it looks.

Sandalwood

Use: Saddle. **Height:** 13.1 hh. **Colours:** All colours.
Identifying features: Small head with straight profile,
short neck, long narrow back, high-set tail, thin legs,
weak-looking quarters, hard feet, usually unshod.

The Sandalwood, bred on the islands of Sumba and
Sumbawa, was named for the sweet-smelling wood
that is these islands' main export. Many have been
exported to Australia for use as children's ponies, and to
Thailand for use as racing ponies. With their good
conformation and delicate size, they clearly display their
Arab ancestry, and are known for the fact that they seem
never to sweat.

Manipuri

Use: Saddle. **Height:** 11–13 hh. **Colours:** All colours.
Identifying features: Long head with broad muzzle,
deep chest, broad body with wiry quarters, short clean
legs, sturdy and surefooted.

The Manipuri is the original polo pony, from the
Assam state of Manipur in north India where polo
was invented 1300 years ago and where it is still played,
albeit in a rougher, tougher form than that which we are
used to. When the English arrived in Assam in the 19th
century they took to polo at once, finding the little
Manipuri ponies ideal mounts, nimble and brave. The
ponies' ancestry is probably Mongolian, and the British
made Arab outcrosses to improve the stock.

Bali

Use: Pack. **Height:** 12–13 hh. **Colours:** Dun with dark
points and dorsal stripe. **Identifying features:** Light
frame with short neck, slender legs and hard feet.

The Bali is usually used as a pack animal, being less
refined than its Indonesian island cousins. It retains
the looks of its primitive type, with its dun colouring and
dorsal stripe, but is immensely rugged and copes well
with the harsh climate and poor fodder of
its native land.

Spiti

Use: Pack. **Height:** 12 hh.
Colours: All colours. **Identifying features:** Plain looks,
thick-set strong body, hard legs and feet.

The Spiti is clearly descended from the vigorous
Mongolian horse. It lives high in the Himalayas,
along India's northernmost borders, and is used as a
tireless pack pony. Its main breeders, the Kanyats, know it
for a good worker even though it can be bad-tempered,
and they have a good trade in the ponies with neighbouring states.

Yakut

Use: Harness, saddle, meat, milk, skins.
Height: 13–14 hh. **Colours:** Any but usually grey.
Identifying features: Thickset head and body, short
strong legs, thick shaggy coat.

The Yakut is descended from the now-extinct Tundra
Horse, and living as it does north of the Arctic Circle
it probably endures more inhospitable and colder conditions
than any other living horse. In winter temperatures fall to
-69°C, and in summer clouds of mosquitoes swarm
everywhere. Those who live in the Yakut Republic rely on
their horses not only for transport but also for meat, milk
and skins.

Kiso

Use: Harness, draught. **Height:** 13 hh. **Colours:** All colours. **Identifying features:** Large head, flat withers, upright shoulders, short body, good legs and feet.

The Kiso is found in the central part of Japan, in the mountains west of Tokyo. It was commonly used as a farm horse, especially in the more remote areas. Horses such as this one are rarely ridden for sport, the Japanese preferring bigger and better horses of the Thoroughbred type.

Kagoshima

Use: Saddle, harness, pack. **Height:** 13 hh. **Colours:** All colours. **Identifying features:** Plain, boxy head, neck level with thick-set body, short legs and hard feet.

The last of the three existing Japanese ponies, the Kagoshima is found on the southern island of Kyushu. Until recently it was thought to be wild. Of poor conformation, the Kagoshima was used by farmers and for transport.

Tarpan

Use: Feral. **Height:** 13 hh. **Colours:** Mouse dun to brown with dorsal stripe: coat sometimes turns white in winter. **Identifying features:** Broad head on short thick neck, long strong back, narrow quarters, short strong legs, oddly-textured coat.

The Tarpan, whose name means 'wild horse', is the last remaining survivor of the primitive steppe pony of Central Asia, one of three founder types of all horse and pony breeds. It is likely that the Tarpan is the distant ancestor of the Arab. The pure Tarpan was hunted almost to extinction, and the modern horse was brought back using close relatives such as the Konik and the Huçul. A semi-wild herd now roams in a forest reserve in Poland, and others are found in zoos. It has retained all the vigour and durability of its ancestors and is very independent.

Batak

Use: Saddle, harness. **Height:** 13 hh.
Colours: All colours. **Identifying features:** Light frame
with straight back and slim legs.

The Batak pony of central Sumatra is widely distributed
throughout Indonesia, and is used as the core stock
for upgrading other pony breeds. Like all the ponies of
the islands, it is economical and tough yet spirited, with
handsome looks pointing to its Arab blood.

Kazakh

Use: Saddle, pack, meat. **Height:** 13.1–14.1 hh.
Colours: All colours **Identifying features:** Plain,
thick-set body with short legs and hard feet.

The Kazakh people of central Asia's steppes keep large
herds of husky little ponies to provide them with
transport, sport and meat as their ancestors have done for
centuries. Today's Kazakh pony has been improved by
outcrosses to Don, Orlov, Russian Trotter and Thoroughbreds
and, while as desert ponies they are still economical to
keep, today they are mainly bred for meat.

Pottock

Use: Saddle, harness. **Height:** 11–14.2 hh **Colours:**
Chestnut, brown, bay, pinto, skewbald. **Identifying
features:** Small head with straight profile except for
small concavity between eyes, straight shoulders, long
back, tendency to coarse legs though strong, hard feet.

The Pottock, one of France's indigenous ponies, is still
semi-wild in the mountainous Basque region where it
comes from. It has few good looks, but is tough and frugal.
As with the Landais, Arab and Welsh Section B stock has
been used to improve the stock, but with less success.
Once one of the pack ponies of choice for Basque smugglers,
today it is usually used as a child's pony or in harness.

Burma Pony or Shan

Use: Harness, pack. **Height:** 13 hh.
Colours: All colours. **Identifying features:** Similar to
Manipuri pony but larger.

This plain little pony is a slightly larger version of the
Manipuri pony, and is bred by the hill people of
eastern Burma. It is strong and willing, but has never shown
the fiery spirit needed to make it a popular polo pony.

Avelignese

Use: Draught, saddle. **Height:** 13.3–14.3 hh.
Colours: Chestnut with flaxen mane and tail.
Identifying features: Small head on crested neck, strong
shoulders, well-muscled deep chest, broad long back,
short legs with good bone, some light feathering.

The Avelignese is cousin to the Haflinger, but is somewhat taller. It is bred in northern Italy, and used for draught work, on farms, and for pony trekking. They are placid and robust.

Hokkaido

Use: Pack, saddle. **Height:** 13 hh. **Colours:** All colours.
Identifying features: Plain head on thickset body, flat
withers, slender legs with some feathering, good feet.

Japan has no indigenous horses, but ponies were
brought to the country in the 3rd century AD by
settlers from Central Asia. Today there are three
closely-related breeds of pony in Japan, all descended
from steppe ponies of Mongolia, China and Korea. The
Hokkaido is found in the northern island of the same
name, where fodder is plentiful.

Mongolian Pony

Use: Saddle, harness, pack, meat, milk.
Height: 12.2–13 hh. **Colours:** All colours.
Identifying features: No fixed standard: usually short
strong bodies and hard feet and legs.

Large numbers of ponies are found all over Outer
Mongolia. They are not generally of a fixed standard,
with a smaller type found south of the Gobi Desert, a
bigger type in the west of Mongolia, and where the
grasslands are better some Don and Orlov blood has
been mixed in. However, all display their Asiatic Wild
Horse roots, and the incredible tenacity and fortitude of
their kind.

Pindos

Use: Saddle, harness, pack, breeding mules.
Height: 12–13 hh. **Colours:** Bay, brown, black.
Identifying features: Long head, narrow body with
long back, weak quarters, slender legs, hard feet
which are generally unshod.

The Pindos, found in the mountainous areas of
Thessaly and Epirus of mainland Greece, is an ancient
breed also known as the Thessalonian. It is descended
from the ancient Thessalonian and other long-extinct local
horses. It is hardy and stubborn in character, and
usefully sure-footed.

Australian Pony

> Use: Saddle. **Height:** 12–14 hh. **Colours:** All colours.
> **Identifying features:** Neat pretty head on good flowing neck, well-formed withers and shoulders, short back and deep girth, good legs and feet, high-set tail.

Australia has no native horses, and horses of various types were taken there by the first settlers. The Australian Pony was developed especially as a child's pony, and it most closely resembles its main influence, the Welsh Mountain Pony. Other influences have been Shetland, Thoroughbred, Hackney, Indonesian ponies, and Arab. A stud book was opened in 1929.

❧ LIGHT HORSES ❧

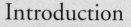

Introduction

Arabs, Barbs, and Thoroughbreds are known as hotbloods, reflecting the purity of their breeding. Other light horses are known as warmbloods. They stand between 15 and 17.2 hh, and in their conformation are suitable for riding. They have a narrow frame and long legs, and the best will have well sloping shoulders, which contribute greatly to a good low action. Here the knee does not rise too high, and the stride will be long, covering the ground economically and smoothly. The back is suitable for a saddle, well muscled and not too long. Most light horses are fast and agile, with good qualities of endurance. Some breeds are famous for their stamina, particularly the so-called 'desert horses' such as the Akhal-Teke.

The nomads of the Steppes, living some 3000 years before Christ, based their culture on the horse, which fulfilled all their requirements. If they came to covet the possessions of neighbouring nations, the horse came to be needed as a warrior's mount; and with the spread of the use of the chariot came fast effective communication. In fact, the horse can be said to have made modern civilization possible.

For many centuries the horse was principally used for transport and as a cavalry mount. However, alongside these uses 'classical' riding was developing, more as an art form than a training for military use. Today its purest form is probably the beautiful spectacle of the Lippizaner horses of the Spanish Riding School in Vienna.

All over the world light horses are used now for leisure riding and for sport. Children join pony clubs; adults hunt, go to the races, and take part in trotting and carriage sports of all kinds. The horse's place in the human heart is assured.

Arab

> **Use:** Riding; improvement of other breeds.
> **Height:** 14.2-15 hh. **Colours:** Grey, chestnut, bay, black.
> **Identifying features:** Fine silky mane and tail, fine short head with large nostrils and wide expressive eyes and a dished face, short back, slender legs, hard feet, short cannons.

Perhaps for as long as 4500 years, the Bedouin of Arabia have bred, lived with and prized these outstanding horses. Carefully maintaining the purity of the bloodline, they fixed the most desirable features, creating an elegant horse of exceptional hardiness and vigour. It was introduced into Europe by the Moors during the 7th century, and was at once desired for its qualities of endurance, courage and gentleness. European state-owned studs took up the Arab in the 18th century, and private studs in Britain followed suit. The Arab is the founder of many other excellent breeds, especially the Thoroughbred, and Arab blood is still used in breeding programmes to improve and refine other breeds. The Arab has only 17 ribs, 5 lumbar vertebrae, and 16 tail bones (other horses have a pattern of 18, 6, 18). This formation explains the shape of the Arab's back and quarters, and its high tail carriage.

FURTHER INFORMATION

• Arabs have great stamina and can maintain a run for over 160km/100 miles or for two or three days.

Barb

Use: Riding; cross-breeding. **Height:** 14.2-15.2 hh.
Colours: Bay, dark bay, chestnut, black, grey.
Identifying features: Long head with narrow forehead
and wide muzzle, giving a boxy shape. Long and
flowing mane, short and strong back with a deep girth
and upright shoulders, small and narrow hooves.

This long-established breed originated
on the Barbary Coast of northern
Africa, where it has existed for many
thousands of years, and where the
Berbers used them in battle.
When the Moors invaded Spain
in the 7th and 8th centuries,
many Berbers joined them,
taking their Barb horses with
them, and over the following
centuries the breed became
established in Europe. It was
also frequently used for
inter-breeding, and thus over a
dozen of today's breeds call the Barb
their ancestor. The Berbers still prize
their Barbs for their endurance and
hardiness. They are very speedy over
short distances, and are known for
their unpredictable temper.

Thoroughbred

Use: Racing, cross-breeding.
Height: 16 hh. **Colours:** All solid colours.
Identifying features: Elegant head on long neck, sloping shoulders, powerful hindquarters, deep chest, hard feet.

The Thoroughbred is the fastest and most valuable horse in the world – the quintessential racehorse. Its line can be traced back to the beginning of the 18th century, when three great Arab stallions – the Byerley Turk, the Darley Arabian and the Godolphin Arabian – were brought back to England and crossed with the best of native English mares, all themselves from long-established racing stock. All modern Thoroughbreds are descended from these three stallions. The Jockey Club, which is now the governing body of British racing, was founded in 1752, and the first General Stud Book was published in 1791. The first Derby was run in 1780, and is still a great occasion.

FURTHER INFORMATION

• Thoroughbreds usually race for about two years, starting as two-year-olds. A stallion with a successful flat racing career is valuable, but once past its racing days, it can be worth millions of pounds at stud.
• Thoroughbreds are courageous, but highly-strung.
• The Thoroughbred has almost perfect proportions and enormous physical stamina.

Budenny

Use: Originally cavalry use, eventing. **Height:** 16 hh.
Colours: Chestnut, bay. **Identifying features:**
Lightly-built with upright, short shoulders, balanced
head with tapering muzzle, well-formed feet.

The Budenny, or Budyonny, was a distinguished Russian
cavalry horse named after Marshal Budenny, who in
the 1920s developed the breed from Thoroughbred-Don
stock at the army stud in the Rostov region of the Soviet
Union. Some weaknesses of the legs and joints inherited
from Don stock, have now been mainly eliminated. It is
now a universal riding horse with special performance skills
at eventing, dressage and long distance events, Budennys
are known for their stamina and calm temperament, and
are a highly successful example of Soviet selective breeding.

Kabardin

Use: Riding, light harness. **Height:** 15–15.2 hh.
Colours: Bay, black. **Identifying features:** Plain looks,
with straight back and shoulders, slightly curved
hindlegs. Some Kabardins pace naturally.

The small Kabardin horse has been used by the
nomadic tribesmen of the Caucasian mountains for
hundreds of years. Sure-footed and willing, this all-purpose
horse was ridden by the tribesmen and also used by them
for food and skins. The breed has been improved by
adding Karabakh, Arab and Turkoman blood, and today
is a hardy, brave riding horse.

Karabakh

> **Use:** Racing, general riding. **Height:** 14 hh.
> **Colours:** Dun, bay, chestnut. **Identifying features:**
> Small head on strong neck, strong compact body with
> powerful quarters and long slim legs, hard feet, coat
> with metallic sheen, low set tail.

Since the 5th century the Karabakh has been bred in the mountains in Azerbaidzhan from which it takes its name. These hardy, brave horses were used for all purposes, but were especially popular as mounts for games such as the local form of polo. They are noted for their speed and sure-footedness. The breed has been crossed with Arab, Akhal-Teke, Turkoman and Persian, and is now rare.

Limousin Halfbred

> **Use:** Saddle. **Height:** 15–16 hh. **Colours:** Chestnut,
> bay. **Identifying features:** Conformation is similar to
> that of an Arab, but more thickset.

The original Limousin was the mount of preference for the medieval French knights, and was itself based on Barb stock. Since then it has been consistently crossed with Arabs and Thoroughbreds. Today's horse is a fine halfbred very close in conformation to a pure-bred Arab. It is a strong, intelligent animal with good powers of endurance.

Orlov Trotter

Use: Trotting, driving, riding. **Height:** 15.2–17 hh.
Colours: Grey, black, bay. **Identifying features:** Small
head, long neck, low withers, long back, broad chest,
powerful hindquarters, hard legs with some feathering.

The Orlov Trotter was developed in the late 18th
century by Count Alexius Orlov at his stud near
Moscow, at a time when horse-breeding in Russia lay in
the hands of the aristocracy. He used an Arab stallion and
mares of various breeds including Dutch, Thoroughbred
and Norfolk Trotter to produce what was in its time the
best trotter in the world and probably the most famous
Russian horse. The American Standardbred has proved to
be faster, and has been crossed with the Orlov Trotter to
produce the Russian Trotter.

Charollais Halfbred

Use: Saddle, hunter. **Height:** 15–16 hh.
Colours: All solid colours.
Identifying features: Strongly-built with good points.

The French are among the world leaders in the
breeding of quality saddle horses, and the Charollais
is no exception. Its original use was that of a cavalry
horse, and its Anglo-Norman and Thoroughbred blood
ensure that it has good qualities of strength and stamina.

Don

Use: Saddle, harness, long-distance racing.
Height: 15.2–16.2 hh. **Colours:** Chestnut, bay, grey.
Identifying features: Plain head, long neck, broad back,
strong hindquarters, straight croup, hard legs,
short straight shoulders.

The Don is the horse of the Cossacks, and is powerful, hardy and reliable. While most of the mounts of Napoleon's invading forces in 1812 died in the harsh winter conditions, the Don endured all. The breed was founded on tough Mongolian steppe horses, with other breeds such as Thoroughbreds, Arabs, and Orlovs introduced for speed in the 19th century. The Don was itself the main influence in the development of the Budenny.

Tersky

Use: Racing, circus. **Height:** 15 hh.
Colours: Usually grey, also bay. **Identifying features:**
Large eyes and straight profile, deep chest, strong
hindquarters, hard legs, high-set tail.

This elegant, athletic Russian horse was developed in the
early 20h century for steeple-chasing, though today
it is usually bred for racing on the flat. The Tersky was
developed from Arab stock with Don and Thoroughbred
blood at the Tersk and Stavropol studs in the north
Caucasus, and has a slightly heavier build than pure-bred
Arabs. It has a gentle temperament and a natural grace
which makes it a popular choice for circus
performing. They are excellent jumpers
and very bold across country.

Karabair

> **Use:** Light draught, saddle. **Height:** 14.2–15 hh.
> **Colours:** All solid colours. **Identifying features:** Strong
> neck and body, short strong legs.

The Karabair is descended from an ancient line of
Russian mountain horses, and is bred in Russia today
less for conformation than to meet requirements for
specific uses. There are three varieties: the Harness, which
is the strongest; the Saddle, the fastest; and the Saddle/
Harness, an all-purpose animal. All of them are hardy and
intelligent.

FURTHER INFORMATION
• The Karabair is highly adaptable, even doing well at
modern sports if crossed with Thoroughbred stock.

Iomud

> **Use:** Saddle. **Height:** 14.2–15 hh.
> **Colours:** Usually grey, also bay, chestnut.
> **Identifying features:** Lightly built but strong with hard
> legs and feet, coat with metallic sheen.

The Iomud is closely related to the Akhal-Teke, arising
in the same parts of central Asia. It has more Arab
blood, and is adaptable and courageous. The Iomud tends
to be smaller than the Akhal-Teke and more highly
strung.

Metis Trotter

Use: Racing. **Height:** 15–15.3 hh. **Colours:** Grey, bay, black, chestnut. **Identifying features:** Small head, long neck, low withers, long back, broad chest, powerful hindquarters, hard legs with some feathering, shoulder rather too upright for good movement.

As the American Standardbred has proved to be a better horse than the Orlov Trotter, Russian breeders began a programme in the 1950s to improve the Orlov Trotter using American Standardbred blood. The result is the Metis Trotter, but as yet the line is not producing predictable foals.

Lokai

Use: Saddle. **Height:** 15 hh. **Colours:** Bay, grey, chestnut. **Identifying features:** Well-proportioned, strong body, strong hard legs and feet, coat with metallic sheen characteristic of so many Russian horses.

The Lokai's ancestry goes back 400 years to the hardy mountain pony used by the Lokai tribesmen of central Uzbekistan. Over the years, so much Arab, Thoroughbred, and Akhal-Teke blood has been added that today's horse looks a quite considerable animal, though it retains all the hardiness and agility of its ancestors.

Kustanair

Use: Light draught, riding. **Height:** 14.2–15.2 hh.
Colours: Chestnut, bay.
Identifying features: All three types have good strong
bodies with short legs and plenty of bone.

The Kustanair, named for the Kustanair region of
north-west Kazakhstan, was developed in the late
19th century by the Imperial Russian Cavalry from the
local wild horses of that area. It was small and hardy,
quickly improved with a better diet and interbreeding
with Don, Strelets and Thoroughbred stallions. Today
three types have evolved: the large Steppe type
used in agriculture; the Saddle type, for
riding; and the Basic, used for both.
It has a good action and is
intelligent and sure-footed.

New Kirghiz

Use: Light draught, riding. **Height:** 14.2–15.2 hh.
Colours: All solid colours.
Identifying features: Short head on strong neck and
body, straight hard legs, no feathering.

The New Kirghiz is the result of extensive interbreeding
in the 1930s between the old Kirghiz pony, bred for
centuries by the nomads of Kirghiz, and Don
and Thoroughbred stallions. The nomads relied
on their hardy little ponies for
transport and for milk, and the New
Kirghiz has inherited all its ancestors'
stamina. Today it is an all-round
horse, known for its good
temperament.

FURTHER INFORMATION

• Much of the hardiness
of the original Kirghiz
pony resulted from
its breeding at high
altitude in the
mountains of
the Tien Shan
region of
Kirghiz.

Akhal-Teke

Use: Riding; competition work, racing, endurance riding. **Height:** 14.2–15.2 hh. **Colours:** Bay, chestnut. **Identifying features:** Small head carried high on long slender neck, high shoulders, long back, shallow body, long legs, scanty mane and low-set tail, fine skin with metallic sheen to coat.

The Akhal-Teke is the descendant of the Tarpan and Horse Type 3, a desert horse with a spare frame and fine skin. These horses were once raced and ridden into battle by the Turkoman tribes of central Asia, where their qualities of boundless stamina and hardiness were highly prized. Their meagre requirements were famous – in 1935 a group of Akhal-Teke were ridden more than 4023km/2500 miles, a journey which took 84 days including three days in the desert, during which time there was no water. The Akhal-Teke is courageous, but can be headstrong and difficult. It is worth persevering with, however, especially for the magnificent movement of this horse.

FURTHER INFORMATION

• The main breeding centre for the Akhal-Teke is at Ashkhabad in Turkmenistan. No other breed contributes successfully to it, although it has itself been used to influence several other breeds.

Plateau Persian

Use: Saddle, cross-breeding. **Height:** 15 hh.
Colours: Chestnut, bay, brown, grey.
Identifying features: Arab conformation but with less
dished face and with very hard feet.

In 1978 the Royal Horse Society of Iran formally
grouped together under the name Plateau Persian a
variety of lovely small Persian-type horses found since
earliest pre-Christian times in the central plateau of Iran.
Included are Persian Arabs, Darashouris, Jafs, Basseris,
Bakhtiaris, and Shirazis. These horses are all famously
frugal, with the ability to survive extremes of
temperature and a poor diet while
retaining all their spirit and
courage.

Turkoman

> **Use:** Saddle; riding and racing.
> **Height:** 14.2–15.2 hh. **Colours:** All solid colours.
> **Identifying features:** Persian in conformation.

This ancient breed dates back to pre-Christian times, and large herds were kept by the nomadic Altai people on the fringes of the Gobi Desert. Today it is still to be found roaming free in what is now Iran. The Turkoman is known for its strength and stamina, and excels at long-distance racing.

Kathiawari

> **Use:** Saddle, harness. **Height:** 14.2–15 hh.
> **Colours:** All, except black. **Identifying features:** Very
> distinctive ears with in-curving tips which can touch,
> plain withers and shoulders, narrow body and
> hindquarters, tail carried high, hard feet.

This tough, light-framed horse had its original home in Kathiawar in north-west India. It comes from indigenous stock, probably founded on Mongolian ponies, with later inter-breeding by Indian princes with Arabs imported from the Gulf States. Today 28 strains are recognized; it is used as a saddle and harness horse in over India.

FURTHER INFORMATION
- Kathiawaris have a tendency to bite.

Albino

> **Use:** Riding, rodeos, circus.
> **Height:** 15.2–16.2 hh. **Colours:** Colourless.
> **Identifying features:** No standard physique.

An albino is a random condition in which there is a complete absence of pigmentation, leaving a white coat, pink eyes and pink skin. In the United States breeders have been developing the mutation as a breed since the early 20th century, with Arab-Morgan foundation stock. They have been successful in producing a good-looking saddle horse with less sensitivity to the sun than most albinos.

Danish Warmblood

> **Use:** Riding, competition. **Height:** 16.2 hh.
> **Colours:** All solid colours. **Identifying features:**
> Thoroughbred-type head on short strong neck, sloping
> shoulders, rounded quarters, nice clean legs and feet.

Although the Danes have had their share of good riders, the Danish Warmblood is a recent breed, its stud book only open since the 1960s. The base stock is Frederiksborg/Thoroughbred, and later additions were Trakehners, Selle Français, and more Thoroughbred. The Danish Warmblood is a superior competition horse with a good action and an excellent temperament.

Shagya Arab

> **Use:** Riding, driving, cavalry.
> **Height:** 15 hh. **Colours:** Grey.
> **Identifying features:** Arab-type physique.

The Shagya Arab is a recent breed, developed in the 19th century by crossing Arabs imported from Syria with native stock at a stud farm in Babolna in Hungary in the mid-1830s. It is named for the Arab stallion called Shagya which sired the breed. The Shagya Arab was once the favoured mount of the Hungarian Hussars, and is now used as a light carriage horse. It is also highly intelligent and good-natured, and looks very similar to the pure-bred Arab.

Pinto

Use: Riding, ranchwork, tourist trail riding. **Height:** Variable. **Colours:** Overo (large patches of black with white), tobiano (white with smaller patches of any colour except black). **Identifying features:** Variable.

The Pinto is recognized as a breed by its colouring rather than by conformation, and can be of several different types. It is a descendant of the horses brought to America in the 16th century by the Spanish, first as Conquistadors and later as settlers. The Pinto, or Paint, was a favourite of the Native American Indians, who appreciated it for the camouflage qualities of its patchy coat and for its hardihood and nimbleness.

Paso Fino

Use: Saddle. **Height:** 14.3 hh.
Colours: All solid colours.
Identifying features: Good head, strong body, hard legs.

The Puerto Rican Paso Fino is descended from the Spanish breeds brought across the Atlantic in the 16th century. It is now popular in the USA and much prized for its three unique four-beat gaits, all natural. The slowest is the *paso fino,* a walking speed; the *paso corto* is slightly faster and is sustainable over long distances; and the *paso largo* is about the pace of a slow canter.

Palomino

Use: Riding (including rodeos, ranchwork and trekking). **Height:** 14–16 hh. **Colours:** Pure light gold in colour with a silvery white mane and tail. Any white socks should not extend past the knee.
Identifying features: Variable physique.

Like the Pinto, the Palomino is defined by colour rather than by conformation. It is recognized as a breed only in the USA, although it is bred in many other countries. Its physique is usually that of a riding horse. Again like the Pinto, the Palomino is descended from the early Spanish horses brought to north America in the 16th century. It is intelligent, and makes a good all-purpose mount.

Quarter Horse

Use: Racing, riding, ranchwork, rodeos.
Height: 14–15.3 hh. **Colours:** Solid colours, usually chestnut. **Identifying features:** Short head on a muscular neck, short-coupled body, broad powerful hindquarters, fine legs.

The Quarter horse is the first truly American horse, and today is the most common, with more than 2 million registered in the USA. In addition, more than 40 other nations own these horses, and the American Quarter Horse Association in Texas looks after the largest equine registry in the world. Quarter horses were bred in the 17th century from Thoroughbreds with Arab, Barb and Turkish stock, the Thoroughbred blood increasing the speed and giving a leaner look. It was christened from the popular 0.4km/quarter-mile races in which it excelled in 17th century New England and it went on to be a valuable ranch horse in the Old West. It is still used on ranches for stock work, and is prized for its agility, strength and versatility.

FURTHER INFORMATION

• In order to achieve great speed over a short distance, the Quarter horse relies on its heavily-muscled hindquarters to help it accelerate very fast.

• The top prize in Quarter horse racing is the All-American Futurity Stakes, run annually in California and worth over 500,000 dollars.

Morgan

> **Use:** Riding, driving, draught, competition.
> **Height:** 14.2–15.2 hh. **Colours:** Bay, brown, black,
> chestnut. **Identifying features:** Slightly concave face
> with large nostrils, thick neck, deep chest, well-formed
> withers and quarters, deep close-coupled body, strong
> legs with short cannons, long mane and tail.

The Morgan is a highly intelligent, good-natured and
sensitive horse, much in demand for leisure riding as
well as for competitions of all kinds. Its action is smooth,
with a dramatic high pace. The first sire was a stallion of
unknown breed (but perhaps Welsh Cob) called Figure,
owned by Justin Morgan, a late-18th-century Vermont
schoolmaster. Figure was enormously strong, and not only
excelled at his work on the farm but also remained
unmatched in contests of strength and speed. The classic
Morgan pose is with the legs extended fore and aft.

Appaloosa

Use: Riding, ranchwork, rodeos. **Height:** 14.2–15.2 hh.
Colours: Six basic patterns of spots, usually on roan or
grey: leopard, snowflake, spotted blanket, white blanket,
marble, frost tip. **Identifying features:** Short-coupled
with strong back, skin on muzzle and genitalia often
mottled, whites of eyes visible, sparse mane and tail,
hard feet often striped.

The original spotted horses probably arrived in North
America with the Spaniards in the 16th century, but
there is plenty of evidence, in the form of cave paintings
and Persian art, to show that horses with this sort of
marking have existed for thousands of years. The
Appaloosa is named after the Palouse River, which runs
through the territory of the Nez Percé Indians and it was
the Nez Percé whose special horse it was. During the
1870s the US Army nearly wiped out both Nez Percé and
Appaloosa, but they managed to survive, and the Appaloosa
is now one of the most popular breeds in the USA. It is
nimble and tractable, and with its attractive dappled
appearance, much in demand for rodeo and show work.

FURTHER INFORMATION

• The Appaloosa Horse Club was formed in Idaho in
1938, and its registry is now the third largest in the world.
• Quarter horses have been used for breeding with the
Appaloosa in recent years, resulting in an increase in the
breed's strength and quality.

American Standardbred

> **Use:** Racing, driving.
> **Height:** 14–16 hh. **Colours:** All solid colours.
> **Identifying features:** Usually Thoroughbred-type, but
> with longer back and more muscular hindquarters,
> croup usually higher than withers.

The American Standardbred is the most famous and the fastest trotter in the world, proponent of a style of racing which is supremely popular in the USA. It springs from an exceptional Thoroughbred stallion named Messenger, imported into the USA in 1788. Messenger's descendant, Hambletonian 10, was a highly prolific sire. Stamina was introduced by Arab, Barb, and Morgan blood, and extra style by Canadian and Hackney blood. It is bred more for its speed than for looks, and is an extremely powerful breed, with iron legs. They trot or pace.

American Saddlebred

Use: Riding, showing. **Height:** 15–16 hh.
Colours: Usually solid colours, but sometimes roan or palomino. **Identifying features:** Small alert head on arched neck, wide nostrils, short strong body, slim clean legs, very high tail carriage.

The American Saddlebred is a most handsome, showy horse. It was developed in the 19th century by rich plantation owners in Kentucky, USA, using Thoroughbred and Morgan stock bred with Canadian Pacer and the now-extinct Narragansett Pacer, to provide a flamboyant yet comfortable ride. Apart from the walk, trot and canter, the Saddlebred has two exclusive gaits, the slow gait and the rack. Both these movements, the latter fast and the former slow, produce a high prance, with each foot pausing in mid-air. All movements are extremely fluid, and the Saddlebred is also noted for its charming nature.

FURTHER INFORMATION

• The high tail carriage is achieved by clipping the tail muscles when the horse is young and resetting them in a crupper.

• The Saddlebred used to be called the Kentucky Saddler and still is in some places. However, it has officially been the American Saddlebred since 1891 when the American Saddle Horse Breeders' Association was formed in Louisville, Kentucky.

Missouri Fox Trotter

Use: Saddle, trial riding. **Height:** 14-16 hh.
Colours: Chestnut, other solid colours.
Identifying features: Neat head with pointed ears on
low-lying neck, powerful shoulders and chest, muscular
hind legs, good feet, tail held away from body.

The Missouri Fox Trotter is similar to the Tennessee
Walker and the Saddlebred. It was developed in the
early 19th century in the Ozark Mountains of Arkansas
and Missouri from Morgan, Thoroughbred and Barb
stock. Originally a good all-round utility horse for farmers
and settlers, today it is mainly a saddle horse, often used
for showing in Western tack. A stud book was opened for
it in 1948. The Fox Trotter has a good temperament, and
a characteristic smooth sliding gait which can be maintained
over long distances.

Colorado Ranger

Use: Saddle. **Height:** 15.2 hh.
Colours: All Appaloosa colours and patterns.
Identifying features: Small head on strong neck,
compact body, strong quarters, hard clean legs and feet.

The Colorado Ranger is one of only three spotted
varieties in the Americas. It is descended from an
Arab and a Barb presented to General Ulysses S. Grant by
the Sultan of Turkey in 1878. The Colorado Ranger was
so named in 1934.

Tennessee Walking Horse

Use: Saddle, show. **Height:** 15–16 hh.
Colours: All solid. **Identifying features:** Fairly large
head which nods in time to the movement of the body,
short-coupled body, powerful clean legs, high-set tail.

Early plantation owners in the states of Kentucky,
Tennessee and Missouri felt the need to develop a
horse which would meet their needs for a stylish yet
practical mount. The old Narragansett Pacer was
outcrossed with Standardbred, Morgan, Thoroughbred
and American Saddlebred, and today the principal
breeding area is still the state of Tennessee. It has three
gaits: a flat walk, the four-beat running walk from which
it gets its name, and a rolling canter.

Criollo

Use: Saddle, stockwork, polo. **Height:** 14–15 hh.
Colours: Classically dun with a dark dorsal stripe, but
also roan, chestnut, bay, black, grey. **Identifying
features:** Medium head with convex face, muscular neck
and shoulders, short deep body, strong legs.

This agile Argentinian horse is the favourite mount of
the gaucho, and is excellent for cattle work on the
pampas. It is descended from the Andalucian, the Barb
and the Arab, brought to South America by the Spanish
300 years ago, and is itself the founder, with the addition
of Thoroughbred blood, of today's outstanding
Argentinian polo ponies. It is a powerful, quick-witted
horse, famously hardy and long-lived.

Mangalarga

> **Use:** Saddle, stockwork, endurance riding.
> **Height:** 14–16 hh. **Colours:** Chestnut, bay, roan, grey.
> **Identifying features:** Long head, short back, powerful hindquarters, long legs, low-set tail.

This Brazilian riding horse was developed about 100 years ago as a lighter-framed version of its Argentinian cousin, the Criollo. Its Altér-Real blood gives it a lighter build and longer legs, but it retains qualities of frugality and hardiness. The Mangalarga has an unusual gait called the *marcha*, which is halfway between a trot and a canter and is extremely comfortable. The Mangalarga is a very good endurance riding horse.

FURTHER INFORMATION
• The Campolino is a very similar breed also much used in Brazil, but rather heavier.

Native Mexican

> **Use:** Saddle. **Height:** 15 hh. **Colours:** All solid colours.
> **Identifying features:** Lean-framed, hard legs.

The Native Mexican horse shares its ancestry with the Mustang, both being descended from horses brought from Spain in the 16th century. Its quality has been raised by crosses with the Criollo and Barb, but it remains a scrubby, hardy, useful animal.

Peruvian Stepping Horse (Paso)

Use: Saddle. **Height:** 14.2–15.2 hh.
Colours: All solid colours. **Identifying features:** Head held high on arched neck, deep broad chest and body (accommodating particularly large lungs), long legs, unusually flexible joints, long mane and tail.

One of several South American breeds all sharing an unusual gait –,the *paso* –,the Peruvian Stepping Horse also shares its 16th-century ancestry with the Criollo of Argentina. It displays great stamina, partly as a result of working at high altitudes in the Andes mountains. Today its breeding is aimed at perfecting the *paso,* which is a natural gait.

Hispano

Use: Saddle. **Height:** 15–16 hh.
Colours: All solid colours.
Identifying features: Good head on strong neck and
body, powerful hindquarters, hard feet and legs.

The Hispano is a good riding horse, descended from
Spanish Arab mares crossed with English Thoroughbred
stallions. It was developed in the Spanish provinces of
Estremadura and Andalusia as a brave, agile sporting
horse, and today is popular in the bull-ring.

Lusitano

Use: Riding, bullfighting. **Height:** 15–16 hh.
Colours: All solid colours, but usually grey.
Identifying features: Small head with straight profile,
short thick neck, compact body and short back, sloping
quarters, long legs with long cannons, full mane and tail.

The Portuguese Lusitano is a close relative of its
neighbour, the Andalucian. Bred since the 16th
century and once an outstanding cavalry horse, it is best
known today as the favoured mount of the Portuguese
bullfighter. The Lusitano is nimble and mettlesome, with
a naturally high action. Lately it has become popular
outside Portugal and there is a thriving export business to
the UK and the USA.

Anglo-Arab

Use: Riding, racing, competition.
Height: 16–16.2 hh. **Colours:** Most solid colours,
especially bay and chestnut. **Identifying features:**
Delicate head with straight profile, withers set well
back, short back and deep chest, rounded hindquarters,
long slender legs, good bone density.

The Anglo-Arab, as its name implies, has been
developed from English Thoroughbreds and Arabs.
Although the British do breed these horses, the French
have been particularly successful in producing good
horses, using Arab stallions and Thoroughbred mares, and
since the beginning of the 19th century have been
working at their famous studs of Pompadour and Tarbes
to perfect these good competition horses. Today they are
sweet-natured, elegant horses, much in demand and bred
in France, the UK and in Poland.

Andalucian

Use: Bullfighting, dressage, parades.
Height: 15.2–16 hh. **Colours:** Usually grey.
Identifying features: Broad forehead and convex profile,
arched neck set off by long wavy mane, deep, short
body, powerful quarters, strong legs with short cannon.

This beautiful grey Spanish horse can today be seen in the bull rings of Spain and at the colourful horse fair of Jerez in southern Spain. The breed stands at the heart of the network of modern horse breeds. The Vandal tribes who conquered Spain in AD 405 brought with them their stocky, tough Germanic horses, and bred them with the local Sorraia horses. When the Berbers swept up from north Africa in the 8th century, they brought with them their beloved Barbs, and added this stock to the Spanish horses. These brave, strong horses were used as cavalry, and were so much prized that Napoleon stole nearly all of them on his Peninsula Campaign in 1808. A few were hidden by the Carthusian monks in Jerez, who successfully founded a new stud. Andalucian blood runs not only in the Lipizzaner, but also in the famous 'dancing' horses of the Americas, the Paso Fino and the Peruvian Stepping Horse. Although not fast, the Andalucian is agile and robust.

FURTHER INFORMATION

• The Andalucian is still principally bred in Jerez and Seville, and is much admired and sought-after.

Irish Draught

Use: Hunting, light draught.
Height: 15–17 hh. **Colours:** All solid colours.
Identifying features: Good plain head on muscular neck, long body, massive legs, large feet.

Once common on farms all over Ireland, this steady, frugal horse is in decline relative to the increase in mechanization in agriculture, and the Irish Government and the Irish Draught Horse Society are working to maintain the breed. The Irish Draught is large, with good strong bone and, if crossed with Thoroughbreds, can produce excellent jumpers and strong hunters. It is the foundation horse of the Irish Hunter.

Altér-Real

Use: Riding. **Height:** 15–16 hh.
Colours: All solid colours, but usually bay or brown.
Identifying features: Small head with straight or slight
convex profile, strong shoulders, short body, deep girth,
hard legs, thick mane and tail, sloped pasterns.

The Altér-Real is a quality Portuguese saddle horse.
The base stock is Andalucian, with some 300 mares
bought by the House of Braganza from the famous Jerez
stud in 1747 to found the Portuguese National Stud,
where horses fit for royalty were to be developed. During
the Peninsular Wars of the 19th century the breed was
almost wiped out by the depredations of Napoleon and
his troops, and in trying to resurrect it afterwards breeders
made many mistakes. However, over the last 50 or 60
years breeding has been much more careful, with more
Andalucian blood introduced, and the modern horse,
though highly-strung, is intelligent and has a good,
showy, action.

FURTHER INFORMATION

• The Altér-Real is ideal for classical riding, and
particularly for *Haute Ecole*.
• In Portugal, mares living out often wear a collar with a bell.
• It wasn't until 1932 that the breed was re-established
by the Ministry of Economy after being destroyed in
1910 with the advent of the Portuguese Republic.

Cleveland Bay

Use: Saddle, harness. **Height:** 15.2–16.2 hh.
Colours: Bay. **Identifying features:** Large head on strong neck and shoulders, thick black mane and tail, long deep body, powerful quarters, strong clean legs.

The Cleveland Bay is probably the oldest of the British horse breeds and, with only a bit of Andalucian and Barb blood added in the 17th century, one of the purest. Originating in Yorkshire, England, in the Middle Ages, it was used mainly as a packhorse but sometimes also as a draught animal. The breed went into decline, and was rescued in the 1960s by the interest of Queen Elizabeth II, who established a breeding programme. This beautiful, powerful horse is now mainly seen drawing the royal carriages on ceremonial occasions. The royal Cleveland Bays live at the Royal Mews behind Buckingham Palace in London. The Cleveland Bay is calm, versatile and long-lived.

Hackney Horse and Hackney Pony

Use: Harness, competition, riding. **Height:** Up to 14 hh (pony); 14–15.3 hh (horse). In the USA, height varies between 11 and 16 hh. **Colours:** All solid colours. **Identifying features:** Small head with convex profile, long upright neck, compact body with deep chest, short legs with strong hocks, tail set and carried high, forelegs with high stepping action.

In 1755, a horse called Original Shales was born, by the great Thoroughbred Blaze out of a Norfolk mare described as a Hackney. Original Shales went on to found the Yorkshire and the Norfolk Roadster breeds and, with the addition of Welsh and Fell pony blood for stamina and Thoroughbred and Arab blood for speed, the Hackney continued to be carefully bred as an excellent trotter, and a reliable harness horse. Originally able to take advantage of the expanding network of proper roads in Britain, it is now exceptionally successful at harness events. The Hackney has a wonderful elastic movement and a courageous nature. The action of the Hackney Pony is fully the equal of its larger cousin.

FURTHER INFORMATION

- The Hackney pony shares the stud book with the bigger Hackney horse, but it is a real pony, not just a small horse. Today it is largely seen in the show ring.

Latvian Harness Horse

Use: Light draught, riding. **Height:** 14–15 hh.
Colours: All solid colours. **Identifying features:**
Powerful, plain looks with clean, hard legs.

Like the Karabair, the Latvian Harness Horse is bred in
three different types for use as a draught horse, a riding
horse or an all-rounder. Its ancestry is the coldblooded
Latvian Forest Horse indigenous to the area for hundreds
of years, but it has had several warmblood crossings
to improve the type. The result is a patient,
hard-working horse, popular throughout
the Russian Federation.

Sokolsky

Use: Light draught. **Height:** 15–16 hh.
Colours: Chestnut. **Identifying features:** Large head,
powerful neck and body with deep girth, straight short
back, hard clean legs and large feet.

The Sokolsky is a native of Poland and is popular
throughout the Russian Federation as well for its
good qualities as an all-round farm horse. It is patient and
strong with a good nature and is willing to undertake any
task presented.

Dutch Warmblood

Use: Competition, riding.
Height: 15–16 hh. **Colours:** All solid colours,
usually chestnut or grey. **Identifying features:**
Thoroughbred-type head on strong neck and withers,
compact, deep body and good hooves and legs.

The Dutch Warmblood was first bred in the Netherlands
in the early 1900s, and has come to prominence since
the Second World War as a most successful competition
horse. It is a cross between two native Dutch breeds, the
Groningen, heavy and powerful, and the Gelderlander, a
charismatic carriage horse. The modern horse has been
further refined with Thoroughbred blood, and also
crossings from French and German Warmbloods.

Kladruber

> **Use:** Saddle, harness. **Height:** 16.2–17.2 hh.
> **Colours:** Usually grey. **Identifying features:** Broad
> forehead and convex profile, arched neck set off by long
> wavy mane, deep, short body, powerful quarters, strong
> legs with short cannon.

The Emperor Maximilian II of Bohemia started a stud at Kladruby (in what is now the Czech Republic) in the 16th century, using imported Andalucian horses. Since then the breed has grown taller, but is still in most ways identical to the original Andalucians. The Kladruber is an elegant horse with good action and a gentle temperament.

Trakehner

Use: Competition, riding. **Height:** 16–17.2 hh.
Colours: All solid colours, usually dark.
Identifying features: Fine, expressive head on long neck, prominent withers, deep chest and strong back with rounded hindquarters, strong legs, hard feet.

Also known as the East Prussian, the Trakehner is a very good and attractive riding horse. It is brave and has excellent qualities of stamina and a good temperament. The Teutonic Knights of the 13th century developed the breed using local Schwieken stock, producing fine cavalry horses, many of which accompanied the knights to the Crusades. Later, Friedrich Wilhelm I of Prussia founded the Royal Stud at Trakehner in what is now Poland, and improved the stock still further with Arab and Thoroughbred blood. The Trakehner is now pre-eminent at show-jumping and dressage.

Wielkopolski

Use: Riding, competition, light farm work. **Height:**
15.2–16.2 hh. **Colours:** All solid colours. **Identifying
features:** Small head on strong neck and shoulders,
compact body with deep girth and medium-length
back, good hindquarters and strong clean legs.

When in 1946 a group of refugees together with
some 100 Trakehners fled West to escape the
Russians, only a few of the stud were left behind in
Poland. Together with two other ancient Polish horses,
the Poznan and the Masuren, they formed the
Wielkopolski, strong, gentle all-rounder with good paces
and a bold jump.

Groningen

Use: Harness, riding. **Height:** 15.2–16.2 hh.
Colours: All solid colours. **Identifying features:** Plain,
strong head on short neck and strong shoulders, long
body, thick legs, high-set tail.

Today the Groningen is uncommon, but in its day it
was a steady, methodical worker in any agricultural
situation. Its roots lie in the heavy Friesian horses of the
Netherlands, together with the strong Oldenburg. It is
still mainly used in harness, for light draught or coach
work, and is noted for being a frugal, willing animal.

Friesian

Use: Harness, riding, all-round.
Height: 15 hh. **Colours:** Black.
Identifying features: Long head on crested neck, full mane and tail, strong compact body, rounded quarters, thick legs with feathering, hard feet of blue horn.

The base stock of the coldblood Friesian is the heavy native horse of northern Europe, known to have lived up to 3000 years ago. Later, Friesians went as war horses to the Crusades. The Spanish, who acquired the Netherlands in the 16th century, brought with them Barbs and Spanish horses, both of which left their legacy in improvements to stamina and movement. Today the

Friesian is known for its pleasant temperament, sensitivity and loyalty. It is useful as a harness horse and is also gratifying to ride, with its fast, high trot.

Gelderlander

Use: Harness, riding. **Height:** 15.2–16.2 hh.
Colours: Solid colours, usually chestnut or grey.
Identifying features: Plain head on strong neck and
shoulders, compact body and long back, powerful
hindquarters, short clean legs.

The Gelderlander was originally a versatile working
farm horse developed in the 19th century and used
widely in its home province of Gelder in the Netherlands.
Crossings with several other breeds, such as the Cleveland
Bay, Thoroughbred and Arab, have helped to refine the
modern Gelderlander, while allowing it to retain its
natural quiet temperament. It is now mainly used as a
carriage horse, and has an especially stylish action.

FURTHER INFORMATION
• Together with the Groningen, the Gelderlander is the
foundation horse for the Dutch Warmblood.

Døle Gudbrandsdal

Use: Riding, light draught. **Height:** 14.2–15.2 hh.
Colours: Solid, usually black, brown, or bay.
Identifying features: Small head on long neck, strong shoulders and girth, powerful quarters, short legs with moderate feathering.

The same prehistoric stock probably gave rise to the British Dale ponies, the British Fell ponies and the Norwegian Døle. Named for the valley of Gudbrandsdal in Norway where they have been bred since the 19th century, they were reliable, sure-footed working horses, capable of steady work at draught or as pack horses. During the Second World War they were in great demand, as in many areas no mechanized form of transport was available. Døles have a turn of speed at the trot, and in 1834 the Thoroughbred stallion Odin was imported to Norway to improve the action. A state stud was opened in 1962, and today Døles account for between half and two-thirds of Norway's horse population.

FURTHER INFORMATION

• A lighter variety, the Døle Trotter, has been developed for harness racing. Originally used for pulling fashionable lightweight carriages, it has been refined with the addition of Thoroughbred and Trotter blood. It is hardy and competitive, while remaining steady and patient.

Finnish

> **Use:** Farm work, riding, harness racing.
> **Height:** 15.2 hh. **Colours:** Chestnut, bay, brown, black.
> **Identifying features:** Short head on stocky neck,
> upright shoulders, long back, deep chest, strong
> quarters, strong clean legs with light feathering.

This ancient breed of horse is regarded as a coldblood, though it is not a heavy horse in the European tradition. The pragmatic Finns have always bred their horses on the basis of performance rather than looks. There are two versions of the Finnish horse: the heavier version is a sturdy animal valuable in agriculture and particularly useful in Finland's forests, and the lighter version is mainly used for riding and sometimes for harness racing. The Finnish is hardy, and capable of working in extreme cold. The light version is fast and nimble, and both are sweet-natured and long lived.

Swedish Warmblood

Use: Competition, riding. **Height:** 15.2–16.3 hh.
Colours: All solid colours. **Identifying features:** Small
neat head on straight neck, compact body with straight
back, rounded quarters, strong legs with short cannons.

The Swedish Warmblood was first bred in the 17th
century as a cavalry horse at the great Swedish studs
of Flyinge and Stromsholm, and today is a first-rate
competitor at dressage, eventing and jumping. It is also
known as the Half-bred, in deference to the addition of
Thoroughbred blood used to refine the breed. European
and Oriental saddle horses were also used in the
programme. It is a sensible and brave horse.

Frederiksborg

Use: Riding, harness. **Height:** 15.2–16 hh.
Colours: Usually chestnut. **Identifying features:** Large
plain head on strong upright neck, upright shoulders,
flat withers and croup, long legs.

Denmark's Royal Frederiksborg Stud, founded in
1562, sent cavalry horses out for the use of armies
across Europe, and riding and harness horses out to all the
royal courts. The horses were a cross between the best
Spanish stock and good German mares, bred originally by
Cistercian monks in Holstein. The export was so popular
that local stocks became depleted, and in 1839 the stud
was forced to close. The breed was registered again in
1923, with the addition of new blood, but the
Frederiksborg is still relatively uncommon. It is a lively,
good-natured horse, with a strong and sweeping action.

Knabstrup

Use: Riding, circus. **Height:** 15.3 hh. **Colours:** Black or
brown spots on roan base. **Identifying features:**
Conformation varies, but white of the eye is visible, and
hooves are often marked with vertical stripes.

Spotted horses have an ancient lineage, and can be seen
in pre-historic cave paintings. Spanish horses appear to
be the foundation of both the Danish Knabstrup and the
North American Appaloosa. A Spanish mare named
Flaebehoppen was brought to Denmark in 1808 by a Mr
Lunn, who bred her to a Frederiksborg stallion. The
resulting line was rich in spotted horses. However, there
was a period of poor breeding, during which the breed

almost died out,
and the modern
horse is closer in
type to the
Appaloosa. It is
a good,
intelligent horse,
each with its
own unique coat
pattern.

Belgian Warmblood

> **Use:** Competition, riding.
> **Height:** 15.2–16.2 hh. **Colours:** All solid colours.
> **Identifying features:** Good head on short neck,
> compact body with deep girth, strong clean legs.

The Belgian Warmblood has been developed since the Second World War, when Belgian breeders crossed their traditional, heavy agricultural horses with Gelderlanders to produce a horse more suited to riding. Later, Hanoverians and Selle Français together with Thoroughbreds were also crossed in to improve the stock still further. The breed now has a good reputation for international competition and excels in the showjumping field.

FURTHER INFORMATION

• Belgian Warmbloods are now well established, and as they are reliably good competitors, have proved a highly successful export for Belgium.

Franches Montagnes

Use: Light draught. **Height:** 15.2–16.1 hh.
Colours: All solid colours. **Identifying features:**
Conformation can vary: usually small head, compact,
strong body, strong legs with some feathering.

The Franches Montagnes is a sure-footed, capable
working horse bred since the end of the 19th century
in the mountains of the Jura region of Switzerland. It is
bred at the National Stud at Avenches, where breeding
concentrates more on character and ability than on
conformation.

Beberbeck

Use: Saddle, light draught. **Height:** 16–16.2 hh.
Colours: Bay, chestnut.
Identifying features: Conformation similar to that of
the Thoroughbred though slightly heavier.

The Beberbeck has been bred at the Beberbeck Stud
near Kassel in western Germany since 1720, when
the original intention was to breed Palominos. The
Beberbeck developed into a good riding and carriage
horse, very patient and gentle. The stud closed in 1930
and the Beberbeck is now bred in only very small
numbers.

Einsiedler

> **Use:** Saddle. **Height:** 16.2 hh. **Colours:** All solid colours. **Identifying features:** Strong neck and body, powerful hindquarters, long hard legs and good feet.

Also known as the Swiss Halfbred or Swiss Warmblood, this horse is a good saddle breed resulting from crossing local mares with Thoroughbred and Anglo-Norman stock. Einsiedlers are bred for their good conformation and are quality all-rounders. They have been bred since the 10th century, and the first stud book was opened in 1655.

FURTHER INFORMATION

• The Einsiedler is considered to be the best of the current Swiss horses.

Bavarian Warmblood

Use: Riding, carriage, light draught.
Height: 15.2–16.2 hh. **Colours:** Chestnut, all solid
colours. **Identifying features:** Short head, upright neck,
strong body, low-set tail, slender legs with light
feathering, sound feet.

The Bavarian Warmblood has been developed from
ancient stock, dating back to the 10th century. The
Rottaler, bred in the fertile Rott Valley of Lower Bavaria,
was the heavy German war horse of the Crusades, later to
be used as powerful agricultural animals. Over the last
200 years, the Rottaler has been crossed with Normans,
Cleveland Bays, Thoroughbreds and Oldenburgs, to
improve the stock, and in 1960 the name 'Rottaler' was
dropped in favour of the new 'Bavarian Warmblood'.
Although not fast, the Bavarian
Warmblood is excellent at
dressage and jumping.

Hanoverian

> **Use:** Competition, riding. **Height:** 15.3–17 hh.
> **Colours:** All solid colours. **Identifying features:** Long
> head and neck, compact powerful body, strong clean
> legs, rather short and with good hard feet.

The great Hanoverian Cream from Lower Saxony is the ancestor of the Hanoverian. The new strain was bred under British royal patronage at the new stud at Celle in Hanover, opened in 1735 – George II of England being Elector of Hanover. At first used mainly for farm work, the Hanoverian was used extensively at the front during the First World War. Since then, Trakehner and Thoroughbred blood have refined the breed, giving more elasticity and rather less power, and Hanoverians are now pre-eminent in the world of dressage and show jumping. They have exceptionally good balance and are brave and good-mannered.

Holsteiner

Use: Competition, riding, driving. **Height:** 16–17 hh.
Colours: All solid colours. **Identifying features:** Elegant
head on arched neck, compact body with deep girth
and high withers, strong hindquarters, low-set tail.

The modern Holsteiner is an outstanding competition
horse. Its 14th century ancestor, the
Marsh Horse of Schleswig-Holstein, was a
heavy, powerful horse bred as a charger.
Later it was used as a
heavy coach horse.
In the 19th century,
Andalucian and
Neapolitan blood
were introduced,
followed by some
Arab and Barb. For further
refinement, Thoroughbreds
were crossed in, and lastly
some Yorkshire Coach Horse.
Today these tall, versatile
horses have exceptionally
good movement and are
often seen competing
internationally at the
top level.

Oldenburg

Use: Competition, riding. **Height:** 16.2–17.2 hh.
Colours: All solid colours. **Identifying features:** Straight
profile, strong neck, long shoulders, muscular chest and
body, powerful hindquarters, strong legs with good
bone, well shaped feet.

The Oldenburg has been bred since the 17th century,
and was originally developed as a versatile coach
horse. The base stock is the heavy Friesian workhorse,
with the addition of Andalucian and Neapolitan blood,
creating a powerful animal well capable of coping with
heavy coaches and rough conditions. Over the ensuing
centuries, Thoroughbred, Hanoverian, Norman and
Cleveland Bay blood have been added, and the modern
horse is now an extremely good all-rounder.

Württemburger

Use: Competition, riding. **Height:** 16.2–17.2 hh.
Colours: All solid colours, usually black, bay or
chestnut. **Identifying features:** Short head and neck,
short body, sound legs with strong feet, thick,
correctly sloped pasterns.

The Würtemburger has been carefully created since
1573, when Duke Christoph von Würemburg founded
the Marbach Stud in Germany. He used good horses from
Turkey and Hungary; then his son added Spanish and
Neapolitan blood; and later Barb and East Friesian. At the
end of the 19th century came Anglo-Norman and East
Prussian additions. The Würtemburger, one of Germany's
six excellent warmblood competition horses, has bred true
to type for over a century. It is a co-operative horse, without
speed but good at competing and hunting.

Rhinelander

Use: Riding. **Height:** 16.2 hh. **Colours:** All solid colours, especially chestnut. **Identifying features:** Short, light neck, plain body, clean legs.

This relatively new breed is based on the old Rhineland heavy draught horse, or Rhenish-German, which is no longer recognized. Since the late 1960s lighter horses have been crossed in to try and create a good riding horse, and with the addition of Thoroughbred, Trakehner and Hanoverian blood the new Rhinelander is proving a useful mount. Breeders are careful to maintain good temperament as well as action.

FURTHER INFORMATION

• By the early 20th century the Rhineland heavy draught horse was the most popular heavy horse breed in Germany, quick to mature and economical to care for. Its demise was directly linked to the decline in the use of the horse in agriculture.

German Trotter

> **Use:** Racing. **Height:** 15–15.3 hh.
> **Colours:** All solid colours. **Identifying features:** Good head, strong body, lean well developed hindquarters, hard slender legs and a good long movement.

The German Trotter is based on the Orlov Trotter from Russia, improved with the addition of French Trotter and American Standardbred blood. It is bred to an exacting standard to fulfil the requirements of the hugely popular sport in Germany of trotting, much more popular than flat racing or steeplechasing.

Selle Français

> **Use:** Competition, riding. **Height:** 15.2–16.2 hh.
> **Colours:** All solid colours. **Identifying features:** Plain head, strong compact body, broad powerful quarters, strong legs with good bone and hocks.

The Selle Français, or French Saddle Horse, dates from the 19th century, when English Thoroughbreds and halfbred stallions were imported into France to cross with local Norman stock. After the Second World War, further crossings were made, with French Trotters, Arabs and more Thoroughbreds, with the aim of developing an excellent competition horse. It is tough and versatile, and especially good at jumping.

East Friesian

Use: Saddle. **Height:** 16–16.2 hh.
Colours: All solid colours.
Identifying features: Straight profile and elegant head,
strong neck and body, light build, short legs.

The East Friesian and the Oldenburg developed
alongside one another until Germany was split at the
end of the Second World War. Since then, the East Friesian
has been crossed with more Arab and Hanoverian blood,
leading to a more compact and spirited horse than its
West German cousin. Today it is a quality saddle horse.

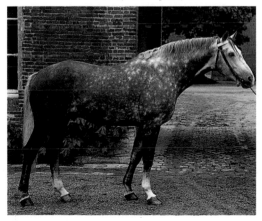

Lipizzaner

> **Use:** High school dressage, carriage driving. **Height:**
> 15-16 hh. **Colours:** Usually grey, but brown colours do
> sometimes occur. **Identifying features:** Largish head
> with straight nose and small ears, crested neck, compact
> body, powerful hindquarters, strong legs, hard hooves.

The Lipizzaner is one of the world's most beautiful and best-known breeds. It is famous for the riding displays given at the Spanish Riding School in Vienna, where it performs spectacular dressage, including the famous leaps called 'airs above the ground'. The School is called 'Spanish' because the Lipizzaner ways developed from five Spanish stallions brought during the 16th century to the Lipizza Stud (now in Slovenia, but then part of the Austro-Hungarian Empire) by the Archduke Charles and crossed with local mares. Today, Lipizzaners destined for the Spanish Riding School are bred at the Piber Stud near Graz in Austria, and fewer than ten are selected each year. The demanding training takes between four and six years, and horses can work well into their thirties. The Lipizzaner is extremely intelligent, strong and obedient.

FURTHER INFORMATION

• Foals are born dark in colour, and lighten as they mature until at about the age of eight they are grey, as required for the Spanish Riding School. There are about 3500 Lipizzaners in the world, and at other studs not all adult horses grow to be grey.

Danubian

Use: Light draught, saddle. **Height:** 15.2 hh.
Colours: Black, dark chestnut.
Identifying features: Neat head, strong compact body,
powerful hindquarters, slender legs.

Developed early in the 20th
century at the Bulgarian State
Stud near Pleven, the Danubian is a
cross of Anglo-Arab mares with
Nonius stallions. In Bulgaria the
Danubian is used mainly
as a light draught horse,
but it is a handy jumper
and a good riding horse
too. It is rarely seen
outside Bulgaria.

FURTHER INFORMATION

• With the drawing back of
the Iron Curtain, it is
thought that more horses
like the Danubian will be seen
in the West.

Pleven

> **Use:** Saddle, draught. **Height:** 15–15.2 hh.
> **Colours:** Chestnut. **Identifying features:** Strong head and neck, powerful body and hindquarters, strong legs.

The Pleven is a Bulgarian saddle horse, popular as a good all-rounder. It was developed from Anglo-Arab stock, and has proved to be a natural jumper as well as being a reliable riding horse, strong enough for agricultural work.

Nonius

> **Use:** Riding, carriage. **Height:** 15.3–16.2 hh.
> **Colours:** Bay, brown. **Identifying features:** Compactly built, with a free stride and good proportions, heavy head, short strong legs, good bone and hard feet.

The Nonius is named for a French stallion of that name born in Normandy in 1810 from a Norman mare, by an English half-bred sire with Norfolk Roadster blood. Nonius was taken to Hungary in 1813, a time when the Austro-Hungarian Empire was at its most powerful, and when the horses it provided were used by the cavalries of many other nations. Some Arab, Lipizzaner, Norman and Thoroughbred blood has been added, and the Nonius is now a good all-rounder, though not built for speed.

East Bulgarian

Use: Light draught, saddle. **Height:** 15–16 hh.
Colours: All solid colours. **Identifying features:** Strong,
muscular conformation with hard legs and feet.

Developed in the early 20th century at state-run stud
farms in Bulgaria, the East Bulgarian is a strong,
versatile horse. The base stock is Thoroughbred, with
outcrosses of Arab and Anglo-Arab, producing an animal
with good qualities of strength and speed.

FURTHER INFORMATION

• In Bulgaria this breed fulfils the functions of an agricultural worker and is also used as a racer and general
saddle horse.

Furioso

Use: Competition, harness. **Height:** 15.2–16.2 hh.
Colours: Black, brown. **Identifying features:** Compactly
built, with a good deep girth, strong hindquarters and
legs, good bone and hard feet.

The Furioso looks very like the Nonius, to which it is
closely related. The founder was an English
Thoroughbred called Furioso, who was taken in 1841 to
the Hungarian stud farm at Mezőhegyes and bred to local
Nonius mares. In the 1850s another Thoroughbred
stallion (with Norfolk Roadster connections), North Star,
was introduced to the stud. The Furioso is strong and
willing but, like the Nonius, not built for speed.
It excels at steeplechasing, where courage
and strength are more useful than
fleetness of foot, and at harness-
racing.

French Trotter

Use: Trotting, both ridden and in harness.
Height: 16–16.2 hh. **Colours:** All solid colours.
Identifying features: Alert head on strong straight neck,
flat withers, short back, well-muscled quarters, long
hard legs with short cannons.

The French Trotter is taller and more powerful than most other trotters. The breed is founded on Norman stock, with the addition in the 1800s of English Thoroughbred and Norfolk Roadster stock. A little later, American Standardbred stock was also introduced. The breed has been recognized since 1922. It is remarkable for its strength, speed, and stamina, and for the fact that, unlike the Standardbred, the French Trotter uses a diagonal trotting gait.

Camargue

> **Use:** Saddle. **Height:** 14 hh. **Colours:** Grey.
> **Identifying features:** Heavy head on short neck, upright
> shoulders, thick-set body, short well-formed legs,
> powerful quarters, low-set tail.

This small horse has lived wild in the marshy Rhône delta of southern France for centuries. It is of ancient lineage, descended from prehistoric horses and influenced only by Barbs in the 7th and 8th centuries. It bears a striking resemblance to the horses painted on the cave walls at Lascaux over 15,000 years ago. Today herds of Camargue horses still roam wild, though they are rounded up annually, branded and subjected to selective gelding. The *gardiens,* the Provençal cowboys, ride the Camargue horses to work the fierce local black bulls, using tack which, with the saddle's high cantle and pommel and the cage stirrups, is identical to that used in Spain. The Camargue has a good action except for the trot, which is so short that it is seldom ridden at this pace.

FURTHER INFORMATION

• Although the Camargue does not have good conformation, the sight of a herd of these 'white horses of the sea' splashing through the shallow salt water at the edge of the Mediterranean is unforgettable.

Salerno

Use: Riding, show jumping. **Height:** 16 hh.
Colours: All solid colours.
Identifying features: Large refined head on good
shoulders, prominent withers, sloping hindquarters,
good legs and feet, long mane and tail.

The Salerno, then known as Persano after the stud
where it was bred, was once the chosen horse of the
Italian cavalry, an amalgamation of Neapolitan, Spanish,
Thoroughbred and Arab blood. It has been bred since the
18th century at the Italian studs of Morese and Persano,
when it was a good school horse with strong limbs. It is a
good quality riding horse, though now reduced in
numbers.

Sardinian

Use: Riding, competition. **Height:** 15–15.2 hh.
Colours: Brown, bay. **Identifying features:** Plain head
on thick neck, long straight back, light build but deep
girth, long cannons.

The Sardinian is a tough, hardy island breed of little
regular conformation. Originally a Barb/Arab cross,
Ferdinand II, King of Aragon, who was adventuring in
Italy at the turn of the 16th century, founded a Spanish
stud near Abbasanta in Italy and sent horses from there to
Sardinia. This stock mingled well with the local horses.
Political changes at the beginning of the 18th century
occasioned the decline of the Sardinian horse, but in 1908
the stock was upgraded using Arab stallions.
Today the Sardinian is a tough, nimble
horse, useful for mounted police and
also for competition work.

Maremmana

Use: Saddle, light draught. **Height:** 15–15.3 hh.
Colours: All solid colours.
Identifying features: Plain, honest conformation with
few distinguishing characteristics. Good bone.

The Maremmana of Tuscany, Italy, developed in the
19th century, does not have a fixed type, being the
product of a great deal of cross-breeding, but it is an
equable, versatile mount, much in demand for a variety of
uses. It is used by the Italian mounted police, for light
agricultural work, and also as a cow pony by the *butteri,*
the local Italian cowboys.

Murgese

Use: Light draught. **Height:** 15–16 hh.
Colours: Chestnut. **Identifying features:** Plain head,
flat withers, short strong back, strong feet, tendency to
weak quarters and joints.

The Murgese was developed in the 1920s in Murge,
Italy, for use as a light draught horse, on stock which
had been bred in the area since the 15th century but
which had almost died out. Its blood contains Avelignese,
Neapolitan and Italian Draught. It is not a good riding
horse as it tends towards a short movement. The mares
can be used to breed good mules.

Indianbred

Use: Saddle. **Height:** 15–16 hh.
Colours: All solid colours. **Identifying features:**
Well-formed head with mobile ears on strong neck,
deep body, good proportions.

The Indianbred was developed to satisfy an on-going demand for an all-rounder for the Indian army, and continues to be produced at army studs all over India. The first British cavalry regiments in India required their men to provide their own mounts, and a large proportion used animals of Arab descent. Later, the Kathiawari was used, until large numbers of Walers were brought from Australia before the First World War. The Indianbred is based on these elements, with outcrosses to the Thoroughbred too. It is intelligent, hardy and willing and bears a strong resemblance to the modern hunter.

Australian Stock Horse (Waler)

Use: Stock work, riding. **Height:** 15–16 hh.
Colours: All solid colours, usually bay.
Identifying features: Physique variable but usually Hunter or Thoroughbred type, strong back and quarters, good legs with short cannons and hard feet.

The first horse in Australia was the Cape Horse of South African stock, brought across the sea in the 19th century. Once in Australia, it came to be known as the Waler, for the state of New South Wales, where it was mainly bred. It was a tough, agile all-rounder, reliably hard-working, and greatly in demand as a cavalry horse, especially in India, and for stock work in the outback. Thousands were shipped to Europe during the First World War, leaving a severe shortage on the farms back in Australia. After the war, Arabs and Thoroughbreds were used to replenish the stock, and in 1971 the name was changed to Australian Stock Horse.

～ HEAVY HORSES ～

Introduction

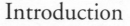

Heavy horses, also known as coldbloods, were part of everyday life on farms and in towns all over Europe until as recently as 60 years ago. Gentle giants, they stand up to 18.2 hh and are immensely strong and powerful. They have a deeper chest and shorter thicker legs than warmbloods of the same height, and their feet are much broader. Their shoulders are more upright, allowing a harness collar to be worn comfortably, and the deep broad chest provides power. The mighty legs and short action greatly increase traction. In some breeds the withers are higher than the croup, which also increases pulling power.

Today's heavy horses are the descendants of the medieval destrier, or warhorse, which although large and powerful, would have been smaller than today's breeds. A fully-armoured knight might have weighed about 136 kg/300 lb, and together with the weight of his saddle and caparison the horse would have provided telling momentum for the knight's lance, which was

anything up to 4.5m/15 ft long. The destrier would have been trained for battle both emotionally and physically by such sports as the tournament.

Since the Middle Ages, the destrier's descendants have been bred for size and power in order to be useful as draught horses. They worked on farms, ploughing the land and hauling carts to market, and they pulled drays and wagons through city streets. Before the invention of the steam engine in 1769, horses provided the only motive power for haulage. Later, they pulled the first buses and trams.

The first railway, which opened in 1803 between

Croydon and Wandsworth, used horse-drawn carriages. Heavy horses were invaluable in the shunting yards of later railways; indeed, the last shunting horse in Europe retired from his work in Newmarket, Cambridgeshire, in 1967.

Heavy horses continued to go to war until the First World War, although as draught animals rather than as chargers. They pulled the heavy guns into position and hauled supplies, as well as drawing the early ambulances.

Today the uses of the heavy horse are mainly ceremonial, as regimental drum horses, though they also pull brewers' drays through city streets as an attraction. They are also bred for showing and, in many countries, for meat.

Shire

Use: Heavy draught; showing. **Height:** 16–18 hh.
Colours: Black, bay, grey with white markings.
Identifying features: Large head with convex profile,
long neck, wide chest and deep girth, dense muscular
body, long heavy legs with abundant fine feathering
and good bone.

Truly the gentle giant of the equine world, the Shire can
exceed 18 hh. Even though it may today have little
agricultural work, it never fails to pull a crowd at a show.
The Shire's ancestors are the Old English Black Horse and
medieval chargers, from the Midland counties of England.
They have been influenced by Friesians and Flanders
Horses, and there is Thoroughbred blood too. Until the
end of the 19th century Shires were called simply 'cart
horses'. In 1884 the Shire Horse Society
was founded. Shires are known for
their exceptional gentleness and
willingness.

Suffolk Punch

Use: Heavy draught. **Height:** 16–16.3 hh.
Colours: Chestnut. **Identifying features:** Large head with broad forehead and straight profile, deep neck on low shoulders, massive rounded body and quarters, short powerful legs with little feathering, small hard feet.

Developed in the 18th century in Suffolk in the east of England, initially the breed was influenced by the Norfolk Roadster, the Norfolk Trotter and the Norfolk Cob. The breed as we know it today, one of the purest in the world, is descended from one stallion foaled in 1768, Thomas Crisp's Horse of Ufford. The Suffolk Punch has good action, and is good-natured and frugal in its requirements.

North Swedish Trotter

Use: Racing. **Height:** 15.3 hh.
Colours: All solid colours. **Identifying features:** Large head on strong body and neck, legs with good bone, large round feet, long mane and tail.

The North Swedish Trotter shares the stud book with the North Swedish Horse but is a lighter Døle cross, producing a horse with a good natural trot and long action. Locally, in northern Scandinavia, they are favourites to race in harness, but the trotters of France and the USA are without doubt faster overall.

Clydesdale

Use: Heavy draught. **Height:** 16.2 – 18 hh.
Colours: Red roan, bay, brown or black, usually with white on face and inside of legs.
Identifying features: Large head with straight profile on massive neck, high withers, sloping shoulders, strong legs with well-defined hocks, heavy feathering.

Local draught horses in Lanarkshire, Scotland, were crossbred in the 18th century with Flemish horses by the Duke of Hamilton and the breeder John Paterson to produce the large, powerful Clydesdale. As well as excelling at agricultural work and timber-hauling, the Clydesdale was invaluable at hauling coal from the newly-opened mines of Lanarkshire. Shire horses were also extensively crossed in, but the Clydesdale has retained a lighter build. Today it is the only Scottish heavy horse, and is used mainly for pulling brewers' drays in cities, or as a drum horse on ceremonial occasions.

Percheron

Use: Heavy draught. **Height:** 15.2 – 17.2 hh.
Colours: Grey, black. **Identifying features:** Neat head
with straight profile and large nostrils, powerful neck,
sloping shoulders, broad body, deep girth, short massive
legs, light feathering, full mane and tail.

The Percheron's famous elegance is thought to be thanks
to its Arab blood, crossed in long ago. The Percheron
springs from the La Perche area of Normandy in France,
where it has had an illustrious history as a warhorse,
farmhorse and even saddle horse. The Percheron is hardy,
even-tempered and has a good action, making it the most
famous French draught horse.

Swedish Ardennes

Use: Draught. **Height:** 15.2–16 hh.
Colours: Black, bay, brown, chestnut.
Identifying features: Large head with blunt nose,
compact body with short back, short, stocky legs with
heavy coarse feathering, short full mane and tail.

The Swedish Ardennes is based on the native North
Swedish Horse, improved with the Ardennais
imported from Belgium. The result is a lighter, more agile
version of the Ardennais, useful for heavy draught work in
cold, inaccessible forest areas of Sweden.

Ardennais

> **Use:** Heavy draught; bred for meat. **Height:** 15.3 hh.
> **Colours:** Bay, roan, chestnut.
> **Identifying features:** Large head with blunt nose,
> compact body with short back, short, stocky legs with
> heavy coarse feathering, short full mane and tail.

The Ardennais has arisen in the Ardennes region
between France and Belgium, where it has been
appreciated for its gentle strength for the last 1000 years.
The modern horse, docile and willing, has been developed
into three distinct types over the last 200 years.
Outcrosses to Thoroughbred, Arab, Percheron and
Boulonnais have led to the lighter Postier; outcrosses to
the Brabant have led to the larger Ardennes du Nord and
to the larger-still Auxois.

Boulonnais

Use: Heavy draught, meat. **Height:** 15.3–16.3 hh.
Colours: Usually grey; also bay, chestnut. **Identifying features:** Fine head on arched neck, compact body with good girth, strong legs with light feathering and short cannons, fine skin, bushy mane and tail.

The Boulonnais comes from north-west France, where in the first century AD the Romans crossed the local heavy horses with their own Arabs. Greatly improved, the Boulonnais proved a useful warhorse in the Middle Ages. It was then crossed out to Spanish horses, to whom the breed owes its improved constitution and action. Today the Boulonnais is a graceful draught horse, not as stocky as other heavy horse breeds.

Breton

> **Use:** Draught. **Height:** 14.3–16.3 hh.
> **Colours:** Red or blue roan, bay, chestnut, grey.
> **Identifying features:** Large head with straight profile,
> short bulky neck, compact stocky body with great depth
> of girth, broad square quarters, legs short and strong
> with light feathering, small hard feet. Tail normally
> docked so that tack does not catch.

The Breton is the local horse of Britanny, in the far
north west of France. There were once several types,
of which two survive. These two share the same stud
book. The larger is the Breton Heavy Draught, arising
from outcrossings to Ardennais, Percheron and
Boulonnais; and the lighter is the Postier Breton, given
better action and less bulk by the addition of Norfolk
Roadster blood.

Norman Cob

> **Use:** Light draught. **Height:** 15.3–16.3 hh.
> **Colours:** Chestnut, bay.
> **Identifying features:** Plain head on strong arched neck,
> strong shoulders, short back, compact stocky body,
> strong clean legs. Tail usually docked.

The Norman Cob has no stud book, but is bred at the
respected studs of Le Pin and St Lô in Normandy,
northern France. At the beginning of the 20th century
the breed was outcrossed to the Norman Draught to
introduce strength and weight to what was at that time a
cavalry horse, and the horse came to be called 'cob'.

Comtois

> **Use:** Draught. **Height:** 14.3–15.3 hh.
> **Colours:** Bay, chestnut; lighter coloured mane and tail.
> **Identifying features:** Large head with blunt nose,
> compact body with short back, short, stocky legs with
> heavy coarse feathering, short full mane and tail.

Closely related to the Ardennais, the Comtois arises in
the Franche-Comté area of the Franco-Swiss border.
It is a smaller horse than the Ardennais, and is noted for
its hardihood and sure-footedness, both of which qualities
are useful for its work in the forests, mountains and
vineyards of its native land.

Trait du Nord

Use: Heavy draught. **Height:** 16 hh. **Colours:** Chestnut, bay, roan. **Identifying features:** Large head with blunt nose, compact body with short back, short, stocky legs with heavy coarse feathering, short full mane and tail.

The Trait du Nord is a larger and heavier relative of the Ardennais, and is the result of the crossing of that breed with the massive Brabant.

Poitevin

Use: Breeding; meat. **Height:** 16–17 hh. **Colours:** Dun, bay, brown. **Identifying features:** Heavy head with blunt nose, large long body, sturdy legs with luxuriant feathering and very large feet, thick mane and tail, tail set low, thick winter coat.

The Poitevin was originally used in the 17th century to help drain the marshes of Poitou on France's Atlantic seaboard. It is the result of crossbreeding Dutch, Danish and Norwegian heavy horses with the descendants of the ancient Forest Horse. The Poitevin has little natural beauty and does not make a good working horse, being rather slow and stolid. Today its main use is to breed, with the large local jackasses, the tall strong mules for which the area is famous and for which there is still demand all over Europe.

North Swedish Horse

> **Use:** Draught. **Height:** 15–15.3 hh.
> **Colours:** All solid colours. **Identifying features:** Large head with longish ears on short arched neck, ample girth, strong legs and sound feet, some feathering, long tousled mane, forelock, and tail.

The ancient Forest Horse of northern Scandinavia is the ancestor of the North Swedish Horse. Much influenced by crossbreedings from Norway's Døle Gudbrandsdal since 1890, when the North Swedish breed society was founded, today the North Swedish is principally bred at Wangen in Sweden. Exacting tests and examinations ensure the good quality of the breeding stock. The North Swedish is a good-natured horse, valuable to loggers and farmers alike for its strength, longevity and resistance to disease.

Brabant
(BELGIAN HEAVY DRAUGHT)

> **Use:** Heavy draught. **Height:** 16.2–17 hh.
> **Colours:** Usually red roan with black points, also bay,
> brown, dun, grey, chestnut. **Identifying features:**
> Smallish, square head, short, heavily muscled neck on
> powerful shoulders, thick, compact body with deep
> girth, massive, rounded quarters, short, strong legs
> with heavy feathering.

This very good heavy horse, today bred mainly in the
Brabant area of Belgium, is not well known outside
Belgium except in the USA, where it is very popular.
Ultimately descended from the prehistoric Forest Horse,
as the Flanders Horse it was once the most famous horse
in Europe, used as a warhorse as well as an agricultural
utility horse. Brabant blood influenced other European
heavy horse breeds, such as the Clydesdale and the Shire.
Today there is little outcrossing, and outstanding qualities
are retained by inbreeding, to produce a horse well suited
to the local climate and conditions. The Brabant is
extremely strong and intelligent.

FURTHER INFORMATION
• The three main lines, established in the 19th century,
are *Gros de la Dendre,* with lighter bay horses; *Gris du
Hainaut,* with grey, dun, or red roan colouring; and *Colosses
de la Mehaique,* the largest and most powerful.

Jutland

> **Use:** Heavy draught. **Height:** 15–16 hh.
> **Colours:** Usually chestnut with blond mane and tail.
> **Identifying features:** Heavy head with square muzzle,
> short crested neck on powerful shoulders and broad
> chest, flat withers, deep girth, massive legs, heavy
> feathering on lower legs.

Descended from the ancient Forest Horse, the Jutland
has been bred in Denmark's Jutland peninsula for
over 1000 years. During this time it has been invaluable
on farms, tirelessly undertaking the heaviest of work, and
in medieval times it thundered into battle carrying
cumbersome, fully-armoured knights. Outcrosses in the
19th century to the Yorkshire Coach Horse and the
Cleveland Bay were followed by the introduction of Suffolk
Punch blood via Oppenheim LXII
in 1860, with the resulting
stocky, round body
shape and
characteristic
chestnut coat with
flaxen mane and
tail. The Jutland is
a docile, gentle
horse.

Vladimir Heavy Draught

Use: Heavy draught. **Height:** 16–17 hh.
Colours: Bay, brown. **Identifying features:** Heavy head
on powerful neck, burly body, stocky legs with good
feathering, long mane and tail.

The Vladimir Heavy Draught horse was recognized as a breed in 1946, having been bred for agricultural work in Russia since the turn of the century. Local mares were bred to Clydesdales and Shire horses at state studs near Moscow, and the addition of Ardennais, Suffolk Punch and Percheron blood have contributed bulk.

Russian Heavy Draught

Use: Draught. **Height:** 14.2–14.3 hh.
Colours: Chestnut, roan, bay. **Identifying features:**
Large head with straight or slightly convex profile,
strong straight neck, powerful body, clean legs,
sometimes with light feathering.

The Russian Heavy Draught is the smallest of the world's heavy horse breeds. It was first bred at Russian state studs in the Ukraine in the early 20th century, and until 1952 was known as the Russian Ardennes. The bloodline includes the Swedish Ardennes, Belgian Heavy Draught and Percheron. Orlov Trotter outcrosses have improved the action and given the modern horse a good, clean line.

Italian Heavy Draught

Use: Light draught; bred for meat. **Height:** 15–16 hh.
Colours: Liver chestnut with flaxen mane and tail, roan.
Identifying features: Fine long head on crested neck, powerful shoulders and broad chest with forelegs set well apart, robust body with broad flat back and good girth, round hindquarters, muscular legs with some feathering.

Since Italy had no indigenous heavy horses, in the 18th century Brabants were imported for use on the land. Later the breed was out crossed to heavy horses from Normandy and Britanny, and also to the Postier Breton, which resulted in a more agile, lighter breed. Still used in agricultural work, the breed is no longer so numerous, and today is often bred for meat as much as for work.

FURTHER INFORMATION

• The Italian Heavy Draught horse has a good trotting action and a lively alert expression.

Toric

> **Use:** Light draught. **Height:** 15–16 hh.
> **Colours:** Chestnut, bay. **Identifying features:** Large
> head, strong long body, short legs with little feathering.

The Toric comes from the newly-independent Baltic state of Estonia, and was only recognized as a breed in 1950. Its ancestors are the local horses of the area, and good outcrossings have improved the breed's size and strength. It is good-natured and biddable.

Noriker

> **Use:** Light draught, riding. **Height:** 16–17 hh.
> **Colours:** Brown, black, chestnut; several coat patterns.
> **Identifying features:** Large head on strong crested neck,
> broad body with deep girth, good shoulders, strong
> quarters, powerful legs with good feet and some
> feathering, very long thick mane and tail.

The Noriker is the utility horse of Austria, and is based on stock brought to the area by the Romans. After 1565 the breeding programme was looked after by the monasteries, and the Salzburg Stud Book was opened. Outcrossings were made to Spanish Horses, Neapolitans and Burgundians to increase size. To this day the Noriker is useful throughout Austria, and is liked for its gentle temperament and strength.

Schleswig Heavy Draught

Use: Draught **Height:** 15.2–16 hh.
Colours: Chestnut with blond mane and tail;
sometimes grey or bay. **Identifying features:** Heavy head
on short crested neck, flat withers, thick compact body,
strong legs with light feathering.

Founded on the Jutland, from which outcrosses were still being made in 1938, the Schleswig Heavy Draught was also crossed in the early 19th century with Yorkshire Coach Horses and Thoroughbreds, and the result is a tractable, strong horse. A breed standard was recognized in 1888, and efforts continue to eliminate faults such as soft feet and a too-long body.

Murakoz

> **Use:** Draught. **Height:** 15–16 hh. **Colours:** Chestnut
> with flaxen mane and tail; also bay, brown, black, grey.
> **Identifying features:** Alert head, clearly defined withers,
> sloping shoulders, good depth of girth, light but
> muscular legs with little feathering, low-set tail.

The Murakoz is Hungary's working horse. It has been bred at Murakoz, on the River Mura in southern Hungary, since the end of the 19th century, when the breed was founded on a Noriker-Arab cross. Since then both Ardennais and Percherons have been used to strengthen the breed. It is the most popular working breed in Hungary to this day, and is noted for its co-operative nature and good lines.

Lithuanian Heavy Draught

> **Use:** Heavy draught. **Height:** 14.3–15 hh.
> **Colours:** Chestnut, with flaxen mane and tail.
> **Identifying features:** Heavy head, compact powerful
> body, strong legs, some feathering, large feet.

The Lithuanian Heavy Draught was only registered as a breed in 1963, having been developed this century to meet the needs of agriculture in the former Soviet Union's Baltic states. The breed was established with Swedish Ardennes stallions on local mares, and the result is a medium-sized horse with great strength.

FURTHER INFORMATION

• The Lithuanian Heavy Draught does not have good action, and seldom moves well at a trot or canter.

WILD AND
❧ FERAL HORSES ❧

About one million years ago the horse family split into two branches. One branch led, via the Tarpan, Forest Horse and Przewalski's Horse, to the modern horse and to today's wild and feral horses; the other led to zebras, asses, donkeys and mules.

Zebras

These elegantly striped animals are found throughout southern Africa. Once there were many species, but today there are just three.

- Grevy's zebra is the largest, standing up to 13.2 hh and weighing in at up to 430 kg/950 lb. They live in the far north of the territory and are very rare, with only about 7000 still living.

- The mountain zebra, which lives in the southern uplands, is also endangered.
- The most abundant is the plains, or common, zebra, which roams the grasslands of the east in large herds. There are seven recognized sub-species, differing from one another by stripe pattern, the most widespread of which is Grant's zebra which accounts for more than 70 per cent of the common zebra population.

The differences between zebras lie mainly in their stripe patterns, and no two zebras have identical stripes. Not even the two sides of a zebra's body match exactly. The stripes are excellent camouflage within the herd. The zebra's large round ears provide excellent hearing. They are speedy and tough, and it is not considered possible to domesticate them.

Ass

There are two groups of ass, the African and the Asiatic. The Asiatic ass has been domesticated for about 6000 years, and large herds were kept in ancient Egypt. In zoological terms it is a 'hemionid', which means that it has characteristics of both the horse and the ass. Its body shape differs from that of the horse, and its voice is distinctly asinine rather than equine. The Asiatic ass, or Onager, is the 'wild ass' of the Bible, and there are many sub-species living today throughout Asia and the Middle East, including the Mongolian Kulan, fleet of foot and hardy, the Tibetan Kiang, adapted for life at high altitudes, and the Indian Ghorkar, clinging to survival in the Rann of Kutch in northern India.

The African ass, originally from the hot, dry regions of north Africa, has been domesticated as the donkey, which is now found the world over, still thriving in conditions most like its arid ancestral homeland. Donkeys usually stand about 100cm/40 inches tall, but miniature donkeys found in Sicily and India stand only 60cm/24 inches, while Spanish donkeys can tower at 15 hh. They are extremely strong for their size, with narrow bodies, flat backs, and legs which may look spindly but are wiry and tough. They have long ears

and a short upright mane, and are known for their characteristic bray. Donkeys range in colour from black to grey or dun, and have on their backs the celebrated dorsal stripe and cross bar on the withers, making up the cross said to have been marked on them in memory of the donkey which carried Jesus into Jerusalem before his crucifixion. The male donkey is known as the jack, and the female is known as the jennet.

Mule

A mule is a cross between a jack ass and a horse mare: a cross between a jennet and a horse stallion is called a hinny. Both mules and hinnies are usually sterile.

One of the most useful working animals in the world since it was first bred in the Middle East 4000 years ago, the mule has been valued above horses for its thrift, versatility and even temperament. They are the most sure-footed of any equine, are nearly as strong as oxen, and are more economical than horses. They are also able to cope with hard work in demanding conditions. Mules have strong bodies with heavy looks and long ears, and are famously stubborn, so much so that their very name has come to mean obstinate. In size they can be anything up to 16 hh.

Mules were widely used for transport in both World Wars, and today's Indian Army still relies heavily on its mules for transport.

Asiatic Wild Horse

Also called Przewalski's Horse, the Asiatic Wild Horse is the only truly wild horse still in existence. It was discovered in Mongolia, south of the Gobi Desert, at the end of the 19th century by a cartographer in the Russian army, Nicolai Przewalski. It became extinct in the wild in 1969, but there are plans to reintroduce zoo-bred animals to the wild.

The Asiatic Wild Horse is dun coloured, with black legs and a dorsal stripe. It has a straight back, heavy head and a short, coarse, upright mane. It stands between 12 and 14.2 hh. This primitive horse is aggressive by nature. Unlike the domestic horse, which possesses 64 chromosomes, the Asiatic Wild Horse possesses 66.

Feral Horses

Feral horses are the descendants of domestic horses which have been set free and which have returned to the wild. There are several herds throughout the world.

• Mustang: the mustang is the light-framed, hardy descendant of Spanish horses brought with the early settlers. Mustangs were tamed again for use as Indian ponies and cow ponies. The very word mustang comes from the Spanish word *mestena,* meaning herd. Once large herds roamed the western states of America, but they did great damage to crops and were seen as an obvious, cheap source of pet food, so were heavily culled. They are now protected by law. The mustang is also called the Cayuse or the Bronco.

• Brumby: the brumby is the feral horse of Australia. Hardy, independent and adaptable, the brumby is the descendant of horses loosed after the Australian Gold Rush of 1851. It flourished in Australia's outback until it too came to be perceived as a pest. In the 1960s huge numbers were shot, and the brumby is now rare.

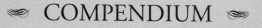

COMPENDIUM

World Records

The strongest horse ever recorded was a Shire gelding called Vulcan who, in 1924, registered a pull equal to a starting load of 47 tonnes on a dynamometer at the British Empire Exhibition at Wembley, London.

• Racehorses are the world's most valuable horses. The most money paid for a yearling is $13.1 million paid for Seattle Dancer in 1985 by Robert Sangster at Keeneland, Kentucky, USA.

• The fastest horse in horse racing over 1.5 miles was the 3-year old Hawkster, who in California in 1989 ran the distance in 2 mins 22.8 sec, which is 60km/37.82 miles per hour.

• The largest wild equid is Grevy's zebra, which stands about 1.5m/59inches at the shoulder and is about 2.5m/8 ft long.

• The smallest wild equid is the African wild ass weighing only about 275kg/606 lb.

• The smallest domestic horse was Little Pumpkin, born in 1973 in South Carolina, USA, weighing only 9.07kg/20 lb.

- The smallest breed of horse is the Falabella of Argentina, with most adults weighing less than 45kg/100 lbs.
- The oldest domestic horse was Old Billy, who died in 1822 aged 62. Old Billy is believed to have been of mainly Cleveland blood, and spent most of his working life towing barges for the Mersey and Irwell Navigation Company in Lancashire.
- The most recent member of the horse family to become extinct is the quagga, which died out from its South African home in 1878. The quagga was a yellowish-brown zebra with stripes only on its head, neck and forequarters. A zoo specimen survived in Amsterdam Zoo until 1883.
- Horses' only blind spots are behind their heads and right below the end of the nose. They have acute night vision, probably as good as that of owls.

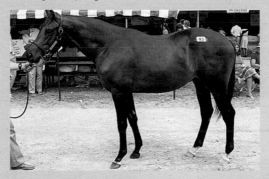

Breeding: the Basics

If you decide you would like to breed from your mare, the first question you must ask is: what am I aiming for? Horses today must fit in with humans in every way, so it is important to consider what will become of a foal, and to have a clear idea of what you want it to be good at and what demand there will be for it. You must have the facilities and knowledge to handle breeding stock – or at least have access to them. Your mare must be suitable for breeding, healthy and with a good temperament and conformation. Any foal will inherit its genes 50/50 from its parents, but whichever genes are prepotent will dominate, and when you are choosing a stallion you should aim for a good animal. Look at its other foals, if you can, to see if it stamps itself on them. Most stallions are registered in the UK, so you are unlikely to find defects, but, ideally, choose one that is registered with a breed society and graded as a stallion.

Choosing a stud may not be easy, as you must find one with a management you feel comfortable with and where these is a suitable stallion. If there is no suitable stud near you, you should look at press advertisements and also talk to other people, at shows and other gatherings. When you have decided, make sure you obtain full details of the stallion you have chosen, and that you know what the stud requires of your mare (vaccinations, removal of shoes, and so on), together with the payment conditions. When the time comes to take your mare to the stud, be sure to comply fully with these requirements.

The best age at which to start a mare breeding is usually four, and a mare can often continue breeding until she is in her 20s. The best time for service is June, so that the foal will be born the following May, just as the weather is beginning to be at its kindest.

Once the mating has taken place, a vet will usually be needed to confirm the pregnancy. This can be done by urine test, blood test, ultrasound scan, or by an internal examination. It can be difficult to tell if a mare is pregnant by looking at her – even several months into the pregnancy mares do not seem very large.

The stud will usually agree to help with the foaling when the time comes, and it is a good idea to accept this help, especially if it is your first time.

It is important that the accommodation for your mare and her foal is very clean and well maintained, with no danger points and some shelter. There must be plenty of space, and the land must be neither concrete-hard nor a quagmire.

Good feeding is extremely important – pregnant and lactating mares need extra protein. For the first few weeks the foal will drink only milk, but by six months it should be weaned. From its earliest days the foal should be handled gently and firmly in order to raise a well-mannered horse. The company of other foals is desirable too.

Showing: the Basics

The forerunner of the modern horse show was the horse fair, where horses were bought and sold. Such fairs still take place all over the world.

The main purpose of the modern horse show, where animals compete, is to encourage improvements in the breed or type, to set standards, and to provide a useful gathering point for owners and breeders.

Under the traditional British system of judging show-ring classes – used at shows throughout the Commonwealth – judgement relies heavily on experience and expert opinion, whereas in the USA and in Europe there is more performance testing against specific requirements.

Under the British system, judgements rest on:
- presence (or personality)
- conformation (the correctness of the horse's structure in relation to the purpose he is intended for)
- ride
- manners

There are various classes:
- children's
- working hunters
- show hunters
- different breed classes
- driving turnouts

In the USA there are also classes for gaited horses such as the Tennessee Walking Horse, and for Western riding.

Horse in Law and Insurance

The sale of horses is like everything else covered by the Trade Description Act, and a horse must be of merchantable quality; that is, fit for the purpose for which it has been sold.

It may be helpful to obtain the advice of a solicitor on any warranty offered by a potential seller.

Riding is a high-risk sport, rated by insurance companies as dangerous as motor racing or mountaineering. It is therefore sensible to take precautions. Some you can do for yourself, such as wearing a good, well-fitting hard hat, with a fixed harness, sensible footwear and making sure you have good instruction in riding.

The insurance of your horse for loss of use or for death by accident, illness, or humane destruction is not necessarily a sensible expense as it can be difficult to obtain payment on a claim.

However, you should have third-party insurance, to cover any damage your horse may do to other people or their property. This is free to members of the British Horse Society and Pony Club.

You should also have insurance to cover the cost of your vet's bills, but be certain to check on the effect on your premium of making any claim.

Horse Health

The horse has a delicate constitution and is susceptible to many ailments. By careful observation of your horse when well you will find it easier to notice symptoms of ill health, and be in a better position to know when to call in the vet.

The temperature of the horse is taken rectally, and should be 38°C. Take the temperature over several days, at the same time each day, and remember that in the case of infection the temperature always rises. A horse with a temperature should be separated from other horses in case it is infectious or contagious.

Horses take between ten and 15 breaths per minute, silently and with very little movement of the abdomen. The coat should be glossy and smooth, with no bald

patches or swelling, and no sweating when at rest.

Observe your horse's behaviour. An ill horse may stand apart from the others in a field, may lie down or be restless. He may sway or swing his head, or hunch his body in discomfort.

A fit horse enjoys its feed, and should not drool while eating. Any loss of appetite may indicate illness. The mouth is usually clean and sweet smelling, with clear pink gums.

The eyes should be clear with no dullness or swelling and no abnormal discharge.

The limbs should be clear with no swelling or heat, and the feet should be smooth with no crumbling or bad smell.

Watch for any abnormal tiredness, lameness or respiratory difficulty.

PREVENTIVE AND ROUTINE CARE

- Worming. Regular worming is important to keep your
  horse clear of internal parasites and to reduce contamin-
  ation of the pasture. One of the most effective means
  of worm control is picking up horses' droppings, which
  should not then be spread on the grass! Horses at grass
  should be wormed every six weeks or so, and it is
  sufficient to worm stabled horses every eight weeks or
  so. The most common kinds of worm to be dealt with
  are redworms, round-worms, tapeworms, and the
  larvae of the bot-fly, though there are other, less
  common types.

- Vaccinations. All horses should be vaccinated against
  tetanus and equine flu. Horses are very susceptible to
  tetanus, and if your horse suffers a wound many vets
  prefer to give tetanus antitoxin even if the horse has
  been vaccinated. Revaccination is usually recommended
  every 18 months to two years after the initial course.
  The incubation period for tetanus can be as long as
  two or three months. The first symptoms are stiffness
  and difficulty in walking, followed by convulsions and
  ultimately death. Once tetanus is contracted there is no
  effective treatment.

- Equine flu is highly contagious, with an incubation
  period of two to four days and horses remain infectious
  for about a week. Treatment includes antibiotics and
  good nursing care, followed by rest to reduce the risk
  of long-term effects on the horse's wind.

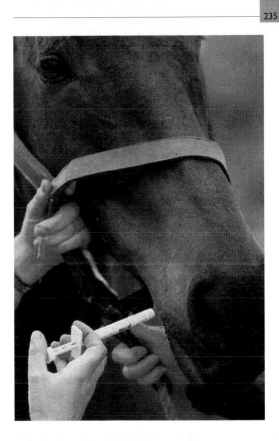

COMMON AILMENTS

Horses are subject to a great many diseases and ailments and a good vet will probably be needed at some point. A sick horse should be kept on his own in a warm, clean and well-ventilated loose box with a deep bed. Offer good food and fresh water, taking away any left-over food and keeping feeding utensils and bowls very clean. The horse will probably like a gentle daily grooming.

There are certain scheduled diseases which by law should be notified to the police or the local authority. These are anthrax, parasitic mange, glanders, epizootic lymphangitis, EVA (Equine Viral Arteritis) and rabies.

OTHER AILMENTS

• Poisoning – poisonous plants include ragwort, laburnum, laurel, privet, yew, rhododendron, bracken. Yew is especially deadly, and can kill a horse within ten minutes.

• Sweet itch – some horses are allergic to certain midges which are active in the summer dusk. Affected horses rub their tail and neck often until they are raw. There is no effective cure, but it can be controlled with careful management. Reduce exposure to midges, relieve irritation with soothing lotion on the affected areas, and stable between 4 pm and 8 am.

• COPD – Chronic Obstructive Pulmonary Disease. This common ailment used to be called 'broken wind' and is caused by an allergy to mould spores in the dust of feed or bedding. Horses with COPD have a harsh, dry cough and can be treated with a nebulizer. Hay should be soaked and bedding should be dustfree.

• Laminitis – once called 'founders', this is the inflammation of the sensitive laminae of the hoof, the tissue between the bone of the foot and the hoof wall.

SILVER HAWK

FIRST AID

A good first-aid kit should contain the following:
- gauze or lint pads,15cm/6 inches square, to use to control bleeding or as a dressing
- bandages, 10cm/4 inches wide and 240cm/8 feet long, absorbent and elastic, to hold a dressing in place
- cotton wool, for cleaning wounds and bathing away discharges
- salt, to make a saline solution (1 tsp of salt to 1.75 litres/1 pint of warm water) for cleaning wounds
- disinfectant, for cleaning wounds or disinfecting utensils and tack
- poultices, for minor wounds
- fly repellent, to keep flies away from minor wounds

Wounds: minor wounds should be gently cleaned with a weak saline solution or disinfectant. If swelling or discharge follows, then infection is present and the vet should be called.

Tendon injuries: a cold compress will help to relieve pain, swelling and inflammation. Bandaging provides support to both limbs.

Colic: remove food and try to prevent the horse from rolling. Ideally, the vet should be called immediately for any case of colic.

Heat stroke: lots of cool water should be hosed over the horse.

Lameness: check for puncture wounds in the foot, swelling in limbs, obvious wounds, loose shoes, stones in the feet, nail wounds. Rest your horse and if the lameness is not better after two or three days, the vet should be called.

Respiratory distress: if increasing the humidity of the air by using steam does not help, call the vet – respiratory distress is potentially serious.

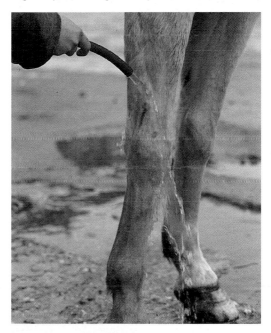

Horse Psychology

The horse is a creature of the wide open spaces, moving slowly in a herd and on constant lookout for danger. The herd, usually consisting of a single family unit with up to 24 members, has a well developed hierarchy, with a dominant mare and her juniors, and a single stallion.

The horse, safer in a herd than alone, thrives in company. Its main defence against danger is constant watchfulness, and this has left it with a nervous temperament. Reactions to danger are first, flight; and if that fails, fight. Thus if a horse is startled it will shy, or otherwise react unpredictably, and may bolt.

This highly-strung behaviour can be overlaid by training, as is the case with our calm, unperturbable police horses and steady hacks. But horses always remain alert for the unexpected.

Feeling safest in company, the horse also needs sufficient exercise taken in a non-restricting space. Abnormal behaviour such as crib biting, weaving and kicking are usually the result of the distress a horse can feel if its lifestyle is too constricting or if it is bored.

Famous Horses

History

Alexander the Great of Macedonia (356-323 BC) was the outstanding military leader of his time. His father bought Bucephalus, a magnificent horse from Thessaly in 343 BC, but the horse proved intractable and could not be ridden. Alexander, who was twelve at the time, noticed that Bucephalus was afraid of shadows, and turned the horse to face the sun. He was then able to mount with no difficulty. From then on only Alexander could ride the horse, and the two rode into battle many times until Bucephalus died at the age of 30. Alexander built the city of Bucephalia in his horse's honour.

The Duke of Wellington, who defeated Napoleon's army at the Battle of Waterloo in 1815, rode his favourite charger Copenhagen on the day of the battle,

staying in the saddle for 15 hours without a break. Copenhagen was a highly-strung Thoroughbred with a tendency to kick, and was famous throughout Britain. He was buried, in 1836, with full military honours, at Wellington's country seat of Stratfield Saye in Hampshire.

A white horse was the emblem of the ancient Saxons, and the famous horse cut into the chalk of a hillside at Uffington in Berkshire is said to commemorate Alfred the Great's victory over the Danes in AD 871. It measures 106m/350 ft from nose to tail.

The famously dissolute Roman Emperor Caligula's horse was called Incitatus. Caligula made his horse a senator and priest and allowed it to be the host at parties.

Buffalo Bill is said to have killed over 4000 buffalo from atop his horse Brigham.

Benito Mussolini rode a horse called Fru Fru.

Hollywood

Tony the Wonder Horse joined Tom Mix in more than 300 films, earning $8 million before injury halted his career in 1932.

Roy Rogers called his horse 'Trigger' because he was so fast and smart. His hoofprints are immortalized in the cement outside Mann's Chinese Theatre in Hollywood.

Champion was Gene Autry's horse in all his films and TV shows. His hoofprints too are in the cement outside Mann's Chinese Theatre.

Literature

Virgil tells us that, after the death of Hector at the siege of Troy, Ulysses had a giant wooden horse made and left outside the gates of the city, giving out that it was an offering to the gods to secure a safe voyage back to Greece. The Trojans dragged the horse into the city not knowing until it was too late that the horse was full of Greek soldiers, who crept out when night fell, and opened the city gates to let in the waiting Greek army.

Pegasus was the mythological winged horse on which Bellerophon rode against the Chimaera. The horse, with Bellerophon on its back, in pale blue on a maroon ground, was adopted as the insignia of all British Airborne troops during the Second World War.

Black Bess was Dick Turpin's mare, and carried him from London to York. The famous highwayman and his horse were created by Harrison Ainsworth.

The children's classic, *Black Beauty* by Anna Sewell, was the first novel about an animal. It has never been out of print since it was published in 1877, and successful films have been made of the story.

Rosinante was Don Quixote's horse, 'all skin and bone'.

In Norse mythology, Sleipnir was Odin's eight-legged grey horse, which could traverse both land and sea. The horse symbolizes the wind, blowing from eight principal points.

Richard III's favourite horse was White Surrey. In the eponymous play, Shakespeare has him command, 'Saddle White Surrey for the field tomorrow.'

The mythical unicorn stood for purity and modesty. Pure white, it was known that only a virgin could catch it. Many medieval manuscripts and tapestries show the elegant unicorn.

Art

The four famous horses of St Mark's, Venice are among the most magnificent equestrian statues in the world. Cast in about 400 BC, for 700 years they adorned the city of Constantinople before being taken to Venice as part of the spoils of war during the First Crusade. For a further 700 years they stood on the façade of St Mark's Cathedral in Venice until recently when they were taken indoors to escape the corrosive air of the late 20th century.

Mogul Horse Dyed with Henna (1740)/Muhammad Fagir Ullah Khan, gouache on paper, Bibliothèque National, Paris (this is lovely)

The False Start/Degas (1869-72), Yale University Art Gallery, New Haven, Connecticut: John Jay Whitney Collection.

Bailed Up/Tom Roberts (1895), Art Gallery of New South Wales, Sydney, Australia. Purchased 1933.

Woodland Encounter/Bev Doolittle (1981), The Greenwich Workshop Inc, Shelton, Connecticut.

Glossary

Horses' characteristics are often described in specialized wording. Here are some common terms and their meanings.

Above the bit: when the horse carries its mouth above the level of the rider's hands. This reduces the rider's control.

Action: the movement of the legs at all paces.

Aids: signals of the rider to the horse.

Blood stock: racing Thoroughbred.

Bone: measurement taken round the leg just under the hock or knee. Determines ability to carry weight.

Breaking-in: training of a horse.

Buck: leap into the air with arched back and landing on stiff legs.

Cannon bone: bone of the foreleg between knee and fetlock.

Chestnut: small horny growth just above the inside of the knee and below the inside of the hock.

Clean-legged: no feathering on lower legs.

Close-coupled: short back, without a hand's width between the last rib and the point of the hip. Opposite of slack loins.

Coldblood: heavy horse breeds, descended from prehistoric Forest Horse.

Colt: an entire male horse under four years of age.

Conformation: the shape and proportions of a horse's body.

Cow hocks: hocks that turn inwards.

Crupper: strap which stops a saddle slipping forwards, attached to the back of the saddle and passing under the horse's tail.

Dam: mother.

Deep girth: measurement from wither to elbow. A body with plenty of room for the heart and lungs within the rib cage. The length of a horse's legs should not exceed the depth of the body from withers to breastbone.

Docking: amputation of the tail for the sake of appearance. Illegal in the UK.

Farrier: someone who makes horseshoes and shoes horses.

Feather: long hair on lower legs.

Filly: female horse under four years old.

Foal: baby horse under one year old.

Frog: wedge-shaped pad in the sole of the foot which acts as a shock absorber.

Gaskin: 'second thigh' extending from stifle to hock.

Gelding: castrated horse or pony.

Girth: measurement round the body, taken behind the withers.

Hands: height of horses in the UK and USA are measured in hands, a hand being 10cm/4 inches.

Haute école: classical art of horsemanship.

Hock: joint in hind leg between second thigh and cannon bone – the equivalent of the human ankle.

Hogged mane: mane clipped close to the neck.

Hotblood: describes Arabs, Barbs and Thoroughbreds.

In-hand: not ridden, led.

Length of rein: the distance between the horse's mouth and the rider's hands. A good length of rein generally means that the horse's neck and shoulders are well proportioned.

Mare: female horse of more than four years.

Nearside: left side of the horse, where it is usual to mount and dismount.

Numnah: saddle-shaped pad placed under the saddle for comfort.

Nuts: concentrated horse feed.

Offside: right side of the horse.

On the leg: a horse that is proportionately too long in the leg.

Outcross: introduction of blood of another breed.

Paces: walk, trot, canter and gallop.

Parietal bones: bones of top of the skull.

Points: the various parts of the horse's body, comprising its conformation. Also in colour description, mane, tail and legs varying in colour from the rest of the body.

Prepotent: tending to produce offspring of marked similarity.

Quarters: body from behind the flank to the tail and down to the top of the gaskin.

Shoulders: the angle from the point of the shoulder to the withers should be about 45 degrees in a riding horse. If the shoulder or the pastern is too upright the horse's action will not be smooth and comfortable.

Sickle hocks: conformational weakness in which the hocks, if seen from the side, are bent so that the lower leg is angled too much.

Sire: father.

Stallion: entire male horse over four years of age.

Stud book: records of a breed society.

Stud: stallion kept for breeding.

Tack: all saddlery and harness equipment.

Type: horse of no breed but which fulfils a particular purpose.

Warmblood: light horses, the result of Arab, Barb or Thoroughbred crosses with other breeds.

Well let-down: the hocks are nearer to the ground, and the lower part of the leg is shorter than the upper. Similarly the front cannons should be shorter than the forearm. This conformation gives a horse more efficient leverage.

Withers: part of the horse where the neck joins the body.

All photographs in this book were taken and supplied by Kit Houghton Photography, Radlet Cottage, Spaxton, Bridgwater, Somerset, TA5 1DE, except: pages 28–9, 79, 101, 105, 106, 109, 111, 116, 124, 131, 147, 165, 213, Bob Langrish; 28–9, illustration by Rick Sullivan; 242, *Fourth Dragoon Guards Leaving for the Crimean War*, by Anonymous (Private Collection). Courtesy of The Bridgeman Art Library; 244, *Ulysses Ploughing the Sea Shore*, by Heywood Hardy (David Messum Fine Paintings, Bucks). Courtesy of The Bridgeman Art Library; 245, *Trojan Horse*, by Niccolo dell Abbate (Galleria Estense, Modena). Courtesy of The Bridgeman Art Library; 246, *Jockeys Before the Start*, by Edgar Degas (Barber Institute, Birmingham). Courtesy of The Bridgeman Art Library; 247, *Scotland Forever*, by Lady E. Southerden Thompson Butler (City Art Gallery, Leeds). Courtesy of The Bridgeman Art Library.

Useful Addresses

Association of British
Riding Schools
Mrs J. Packer
Old Brewery Yard
Penzance
Cornwall TR18 2SL

British Horse Society
British Equestrian Centre
Stoneleigh
Kenilworth
Warwickshire CV8 2LR

Horse & Hound Magazine
King's Reach Tower
Stamford Street
London SE1 9LS

National Pony Society
Willingdon House
102 High Street
Alton
Hampshire GU34 1EN

Riding for the Disabled
Association
National Agricultural
Centre
Stoneleigh
Kenilworth
Warwickshire CV8 2LR

Royal College of Veterinary
Surgeons
32 Belgrave Square
London SW1X 9QP

International League for
the Protection of Horses
Colvin House
Hall Farm
Shetterton
Norwich
Norfolk NR16 2LR
Tel: 01953 498682

British Equestrian Directory
Equestrian Management
Consultants Ltd
Wothersome Grange
Bramham
Wetherby
West Yorkshire LS23 6LY

The Equine Nutrition
Society
Woodlands
Cadsden
Princes Risborough
Bucks HP17 0NB

Index

COLLINS GEM

Bestselling Collins Gem titles include:

Gem English Dictionary (£3.99)

Gem Thesaurus (£3.99)

Gem French Dictionary (£3.99)

Gem German Dictionary (£3.99)

Gem Calorie Counter (£2.99)

Gem Basic Facts Mathematics (£3.50)

Gem SAS Survival Guide (£3.99)

Gem Babies' Names (£2.99)

Gem Card Games (£3.50)

Gem Ready Reference (£3.50)

All Collins Gems are available from your local bookseller or can be ordered directly from the publishers.

In the UK, contact Mail Order, Dept 2A, HarperCollins Publishers, Westerhill Rd, Bishopbriggs, Glasgow, G64 2QT, listing the titles required and enclosing a cheque or p.o. for the value of the books plus £1.00 for the first title and 25p for each additional title to cover p&p. Access and Visa cardholders can order on 0141-772 2281 (24 hr).

In Australia, contact Customer Services, HarperCollins Distribution, Yarrawa Rd, Moss Vale 2577 (tel. [048] 68 0300). **In New Zealand**, contact Customer Services, HarperCollins Publishers, 31 View Rd, Glenfield, Auckland 10 (tel. [09] 444 3740). **In Canada**, contact your local bookshop.

All prices quoted are correct at time of going to press.

COLLINS